City as Memory

City as Memory

A SHORT BIOGRAPHY OF SRINAGAR

SADAF WANI

ALEPH

ALEPH BOOK COMPANY
An independent publishing firm
promoted by *Rupa Publications India*

First published in India in 2024
by Aleph Book Company
7/16 Ansari Road, Daryaganj
New Delhi 110 002

Copyright © Sadaf Wani 2024

The author has asserted her moral rights.

All rights reserved.

The views and opinions expressed in this book are those of the author and the facts are as reported by her, which have been verified to the extent possible, and the publisher is not in any way liable for the same.

The publisher has used its best endeavours to ensure that URLs for external websites referred to in this book are correct and active at the time of going to press. However, the publisher has no responsibility for the websites and can make no guarantee that a site will remain live or that the content is or will remain appropriate.

No part of this publication may be reproduced, transmitted, or stored in a retrieval system, in any form or by any means, without permission in writing from Aleph Book Company.

ISBN: 978-81-19635-68-9

1 3 5 7 9 10 8 6 4 2

Printed in India

This book is sold subject to the condition that it shall not, by way of trade or otherwise, be lent, resold, hired out, or otherwise circulated without the publisher's prior consent in any form of binding or cover other than that in which it is published.

*For Nazir and Mehjabeen who've shown me
the nurturing power of unconditional love;
for feminist solidarities that form the
ground that I stand on; and
for Kashmir, the only home that there is.*

A NOTE ON THE BOOK

To reflect the native pronunciations of names, the book uses Kashmiri spellings. Moreover, several names of people have been anonymized to protect the identities of those who have shared their experiences.

The city, however, does not tell its past, but contains it like the lines of a hand, written in the corners of the streets, the gratings of the windows, the banisters of the steps, the antennae of the lightning rods, the poles of the flags, every segment marked in turn with scratches, indentations, scrolls.

Italo Calvino, *Invisible Cities*

CONTENTS

Before We Begin 1

'It's Pronounced Sirinagar' 18

Between Shahr-e-Khas and Downtown 49

(Un)Belonging in the Shahr 80

Pale Hands That Love Beside the Shalimar 120

Acknowledgements 161

Notes 165

BEFORE WE BEGIN

When I was tasked with writing this book, which was to be my first full-length work, the email with the publishing offer filled me with a sense of euphoric fulfilment that one would expect any aspiring young writer to feel when approached by a beloved publishing house. However, as soon I sent off the mail agreeing to the offer, the joy wafted away, leaving in its place familiar feelings of self-doubt and anxiety. Why should I be writing about Srinagar? Why should I be imposing my version of the city as a generalized biography of the place? I tried to rationalize the answers to these questions by thinking about my personal associations and professional engagements with the city, but even then, I was still not fully convinced as to why this imposition would be fair. That is until I came across Joan Didion's essay, *Why I Write*, buried deep within the recesses of my Pocket app. In the essay Didion writes, 'In many ways, writing is the act of saying I, of imposing oneself upon other people, of saying *listen to me, see it my way, change your mind*. It's an aggressive, even a hostile act. You can disguise its aggressiveness all you want with veils of subordinate clauses and qualifiers and tentative subjunctives, with ellipses and evasions—with the whole manner of intimating rather than claiming, of alluding rather than stating—but there's no getting around the fact that setting words on paper is the tactic of a secret bully, an invasion, an imposition of the writer's sensibility on the reader's most private space.'

Didion's essay resolved my apprehensions by clarifying that my concerns were not specific to my writings or writings on cities. The act of imposition is, in fact, central to the very act of writing, and in a way, it contributes to the thrill of it. It is about the reader inviting you into their mind, granting you access to their most intimate thoughts, beliefs, and biases. In this silent pact, they hand you the power to disrupt their preconceived notions, by letting you selectively challenge, solidify, and rewire their mind and the perceptions they hold dear.

Now that this question was out of the way, I needed some conceptual clarity on what was going to be my agenda for writing this book. In our earlier conversations, my editor had mentioned that like other books in the series, this book should compel the reader to visit the city. But in all honesty, I have never wanted to write a book that would prompt a dissociated reader from a faraway place to land up in a city central to my homeland. Then was I going to write this book to give the people of my homeland, and others, a brief overview of the political and humanitarian injustices done to them in the recent and distant past? I found myself mentally and emotionally incapable of taking on this responsibility.

My younger self in all her naivety had tried to

city as memory

theorize and when that came crashing down, therapize, the collective experiences of 13.6 million people back home. In the summer of 2019, months before Article 370 was revoked in Jammu and Kashmir, I had found myself sitting in therapy sessions, forewarning my therapist that something ominous was coming, and I could feel it in my bones. After August, the storm had subsided, and like everyone else, I also kept looking through the wreckage to find the word that would describe that experience of seeing your reality being altered. Disillusioned by psychotherapy's limitations in addressing mass political events and weary of the relentless and aggressive mainstream discourse on Kashmir, I gave up all attempts to seek external help in navigating my lived reality. Instead, I undertook a solo travel through different stages of grief, before building myself a cozy campsite on the metaphorical stage of depressive numbness.

When this book came along, I tried to move forward or backwards, but like millions of my people, I found myself stuck. This book has been written from that position of *stuckness*, where I don't know where the collective future or the aspirations for it are headed, and I can't make sense of the present entirely. I can only keep my eyes open and witness the changes to the geography, demography, and the idea of Kashmir.

Since none of the metanarratives that could cover the city in broad strokes made sense, I found myself looking keenly at the smaller, intimate fragments through which I knew the place: its people. So, this book is primarily about the people and the lifeworlds they inhabit in Srinagar. Millions of these lifeworlds come together and intertwine, sometimes harmoniously in agreement, and other times clashing in contradiction, creating in their juxtaposition, a fascinating mosaic of lifeworlds called Shahr-e-Sirinagar. As I stared at the mosaic of the city, I wanted to adopt a position of neutrality and extend equal importance to all individual units of this mosaic and to all the lifeworlds in the city. However, my ambitions were immediately cut short by my limited accessibility and lack of familiarity with the vast array of lifeworlds comprising the city. So, moving forward necessitated deep introspection, forcing me to confront my own limitations and personal associations with Srinagar.

I have barely stayed in the city for periods long enough to claim to have read the 'pulse of the city'—if there is such a singular entity at all. However, my association with Srinagar has remained constant over the past three decades, even as the prism through which I have seen the city has kept changing. Srinagar first came to me as the city of my father's youth—his matamaal (maternal home) and the city where he spent his adolescence and subsequent years in government services as a young civil engineer in the PWD department. In my teenage years, Srinagar came to me as the long one-and-a-half-hour journey from Varmul to see my cousins and also as a dull alternative that my parents

city as memory

would resort to for family picnics when they didn't want to take us to Gulmarg, Pahalgam, or Sonmarg. Even as I would frown, sigh, and cry, I found myself standing in front of the water fountains at the Shalimar Bagh begrudgingly posing for photographs with my siblings every summer. For most of my twenties and particularly the last seven years, Srinagar has been the face of Kashmir every time I have engaged with Kashmir as a subject of my anthropological inquiry. Srinagar and its historically changing forms have been the centre of political, administrative, and cultural activity for Kashmir for centuries and because of this prominence, even with staggered documentation, Srinagar is one of the better-researched areas of Kashmir. This professional association with Srinagar has allowed me the flexibility of changing my lens towards the city, and every time my research questions have changed, Srinagar has revealed its entirely different sides in response to my curiosities.

Growing up in Varmul in the late 90s, I spent a lot of time indoors. Going out was a rare event, and the reasons for this confinement were many—the weather was too cold, public spaces were intensely militarized, my parents were not very social, and not much happened in the city. So, whenever I got to step out even for a thirty-minute drive to Sopore or for a shopping visit to Srinagar, a strong sense of freedom overtook me. I wanted to see everything around me, note it down in my journal, capture the sounds, cut out the scenes of everyday social exchanges and take them home with me, so that they would accompany me during those infinitely long nights of excruciating boredom. The digital camera came as the technological manifestation of my prayers, as it allowed me to cut out visual slices from an ongoing continuous reality, freeze them, and pack them as a complete moment that I could take home. Hence, Srinagar is registered in my head as a series of frames, each of which led to stories that I could have explored if the car had stopped moving for a bit.

This book came as an opportunity to pick up some of those frames and explore the stories behind them. It legitimized my curiosities and intrusions into the lives of people around me. During the process of writing it, I tried to use my sociological training to divide and segment the city into parts for my anthropological inquiry. While the segments that I constructed in my previous drafts fell into (somewhat) consistent sociological themes, the sense of detachment with which I had to talk about a piece of my homeland, made the writing alien and the book, not mine. Of all the stories I heard, I could not get myself to theorize their experiences, and arrange them in neat paragraphs where I try to establish a semblance of rationality or chronological order to explain what has been happening in the city, for a lot of that has been madness, that has not made sense to Kashmir and Kashmiris.

My search for a framework for the book led me back in time to 2013, to my Philosophy class at Hindu College where I remember being mind-blown by my

city as memory

course on Continental Philosophy. Coming from the sciences, a lot of what was taught in the course did not make much sense to me until I came across papers on continental philosophy. I leafed through the texts of prominent figures of continental philosophy like Søren Aabye Kierkegaard, Simone de Beauvoir, Jean-Paul Sartre, Friedrich Nietzsche, and I absorbed their existential fatigue like a sponge. Growing up in the aftermath of insurgency in Kashmir, the precarity of life in the face of violent conflict meant that life and death existed in polar opposition to each other in my head, where life=safety=good and death=(untimely) loss=bad. This was until my studies exposed me to a bunch of affluent white men who had the socio-political stability, economic support systems, and intellectual calibre to ask questions such as why is life so good after all? From 2008 onwards Kashmir saw a mass shift from armed militancy to large-scale street protests and demonstrations. Triggered by the public outcry over the land transfer to the Shri Amarnathji Shrine Board in 2008, Kashmir witnessed protest gatherings on an unprecedented scale, with some rallies drawing as many as 20,000 protestors. The confrontations that ensued with the armed forces during these rallies left around sixty-three demonstrators dead. The events of 2008 established an ominous blueprint for all protest movements and state responses to it for the next decade, with some of the worst spikes happening in 2009 (following the Shopian rape and murder case), 2010 (as a consequence of the Machil fake encounter row), 2011 (after the death of Tufail Mattoo), 2013 (in the wake of Afzal Guru's hanging), and 2016–17 (in the aftermath of Burhan Wani's killing). As the situation in Kashmir deteriorated, unable to find a way forward, I found solace in taking ten steps backward, by immersing myself in abstractions and vague ethical dilemmas. Delving into philosophical introspections helped me relegate conflict and its associated traumas to the deep corners of my consciousness. This was until I came home in my third year of undergraduation, and I was caught in a stone pelting–tear gas exchange between the security forces and protestors. As tear gas entered my eyes and gut, the threads of existential angst in my mind rearranged themselves to reveal life=good, death=bad.

I took the sign and understood that the questions that excited these philosophers I so adored were not so relevant to my life. It made me feel less of an intellectual, but I could no longer sit in the class and find meaning in questioning the existence of my desk and my sensory perception of it, because every time I sneaked a look at my phone in class, the death statistics of protestors kept ticking. The table was real, the city was real, the homeland was real, and the boys who were dying were real too. The grief on the faces of their family members and the crushing sensation that I felt in my chest when I saw the pictures of their bodies being taken away was real too. I heard grand ideas surrounding questions of thought, reason, violence, and existence, but none of them addressed the immediacy of what I was going through. The suffocation inside my chest which I had tried to attribute to unresolved abstract introspections, was slowly revealing that its triggers, in fact, were very material. My attempts to create a contextless world of ideas that would unify me with the philosophers from the past were time and again being punctured by my geopolitical context, and local words that I had so hated: curfew, pellet guns, baktarband (armoured vehicles used by security forces), dheel (a brief span of relaxation during curfews), tear gas, hartal (a public shutdown or strike). I began to wonder if Immanuel Kant had lived in Kashmir and his disciplined walks were as disrupted by curfews as mine, and if he were locked inside his house with his family for an infinite amount of time, while stones, tear gas, and death made the rounds outside his windows, would he have still written the *Critique of Pure Reason*?

However, not all was lost to disillusionment. The crisis of my early youth paid off, for Edmund Husserl and Alfred Schutz came back from the pits of my subconsciousness and helped me look at the numerous stories emerging out of Srinagar through their framework of 'lifeworlds'*. This allowed me to look at

---

*Simply put, 'Lifeworld' (German: 'Lebenswelt') is a central concept in phenomenology that emphasizes that perception of external reality is shaped by the mind's engagement with it. Rather than viewing the world as an objective entity to be decoded, it places

the narratives from the city not as mere examples that can be used to substantiate my research claims and analysis, but as whole worlds on their own. It also allowed me to write about the city without making any objective claims to define the city in a certain way. Instead, I have anthologized certain stories where the narrators have shared their subjective experiences of the city that have become the formative basis of their association with Srinagar.

I took this divergence into my own life for two reasons. Firstly, to give you a brief glimpse of what my lifeworlds are like and what could be the preferences and biases that would have influenced my experiences and interpretations of the city. Since I have undertaken the task of walking you through Srinagar, we both must move forward with this awareness that the Srinagar we are walking through is an extension of my spatial and affective bonds with the city, and the biography of the city that I have mapped is my version of the city. This version is one of the millions of lifeworlds that are based around the myth and the truth of Srinagar, and the harmony or discord of this portrayal with other versions of the city will always be mediated by a spool of variables across social identities and personal

---

significant importance on our perception, individual experiences, cultural backgrounds, and beliefs in shaping reality. In this view, rather than being passively received, reality is interpreted through the active interplay between the mind and external occurrences.

experiences. Secondly, I spoke about instances from my own life to show how any account from Kashmir especially after the 1990s, however seemingly apolitical, is always responding to the political and humanitarian crisis in Kashmir. These crises permeate into our daily existence, affecting our most private thoughts, feelings, and choices, whether we are conscious of it or not. So no account of Kashmir can be written without talking about the everyday implications of its turbulent political history. By extension, Srinagar cannot be read as a *normal* city; it has been a city of turmoil. While overtly political, the implications of this conflict extend to the cultural, experiential, and affective spheres of life in Srinagar and therefore seep into all readings and accounts of the city.

The most basic assurance provided by *normal* cities is the experience of safety and functionality for a majority of their inhabitants on an everyday basis. It is upon the foundation of this basic minimum stability that the market economy operates, social and cultural exchanges flourish, and the essence of an urban city is constructed. Srinagar has been unable to hold this pact of safety and security for more than the past four decades. In its place, it has given its inhabitants a precarious normalcy—a normalcy that is not sure of its own lifespan, which can get disrupted anytime through violence or fears of violence. This state of extended precarity is not a reaction to a singular traumatic event but rather is a manifestation of a pervasive culture of uncertainty and disruptions in civic functions and liberties that has become a part of people's lived experience in the city. Its impact extends across various facets of life, influencing experiences of urbanity, employment, leisure, cultural production, popular culture, visual language, collective imagination, and every conceivable aspect that collectively defines the essence of a city.

While absent in most written accounts of the city, this precarity is preserved in inconspicuous corners of the city—in the material and visual elements of the city, as well as in the narratives of daily life within it. Visual indicators of unrest, such as street art, shattered window panes, and defaced billboards endure beyond the more immediate signs of violence, like the sounds of bullets and pellet guns, slogans and chants, and the smell of tear gas. For those perceptive to the city's history, these signs manifest ubiquitously. Similarly, for those willing to listen, the personal narratives of inhabitants reveal the humanitarian toll of the conflict in Kashmir and how the city has exhibited perseverance in the face of it. Instead of treating such accounts as exceptional accounts from the city's periphery, they need to be acknowledged as integral threads weaving the story of Srinagar.

Yet, it is crucial to recognize that the violent political conflict is a recent addition to the city's story. Founded in the sixth century, the city possesses a rich history that has been overshadowed by its tumultuous present. Despite existing for over 2,000 years, only selective events such as Kashmir's accession to India in 1947 and the rise of local militancy movements in 1989 have come to define the city's contemporary narrative. During the partition of the Indian mainland in 1947, Jammu and Kashmir existed as a Muslim-majority princely state ruled by a Hindu Dogra ruler, Hari Singh. Seeking to maintain Kashmir's independence, he proposed signing standstill agreements with both India and Pakistan. However, following a tribal invasion of Pathan raiders from Pakistan, he sought India's help in defending his territory. India agreed to assist him under the condition that Kashmir accede to India. Subsequently, Hari Singh signed the Instrument of Accession in October 1947, surrendering only defense, external affairs, and communications to India, while retaining a separate constituent assembly to frame a distinct constitution for Jammu and Kashmir.

The partition of British India into India and Pakistan happened primarily along religious lines, with most Hindus settling in India and the Muslim community moving to Pakistan. The alignment of the Muslim-majority state of Kashmir with India was contrary to this logic of territorial and demographic division based on religion. Since 1947, India and Pakistan have engaged in fierce contestations over the validity of the Instrument of Accession and the nature of Kashmir's accession to India. This contestation, combined with other factors, has manifested in three full-blown wars between the two countries, with periods after marked by hostility and military threats. Following the first Kashmir war in 1947–48, India's prime minister, Pandit Jawaharlal Nehru, took the Kashmir dispute to the United Nations in 1948. The UN mediated a ceasefire line, splitting the princely state of Jammu and Kashmir between India and Pakistan. One-third of the territory was attributed as a semi-autonomous entity to Pakistan known as Azad Jammu and Kashmir (AJK) in Pakistan and Pakistan-occupied Kashmir (POK) in India. Two-thirds of the territory, including the valley of Kashmir, came under Indian control. In 1948, the United Nations Security Council Resolution 39 was passed, offering to mediate the dispute by setting up a commission comprising three members, one from India, one from Pakistan, and the third chosen by both India and Pakistan to settle the dispute. The UN also set up the United Nations Commission for India and Pakistan (UNCIP) to investigate and mediate the dispute between the two countries. In 1949, UNCIP recommended handing over the region to a quasi-sovereign power of the plebiscite administrator. However, the recommendations did not materialize because of disagreements between India and Pakistan.

Amidst these contestations, Kashmiris have long demanded sovereignty as an option, reflecting their desire for nationhood, a struggle dating back to before India and Pakistan existed as separate countries. Between 1947 and 1989, Kashmir witnessed many attempts to politically consolidate demands for territorial and political sovereignty. However, factors including alleged election rigging by the Indian government in 1987 contributed to mass disillusionment with conventional political processes. In 1989, the struggle for sovereignty turned violent, leading to a militant insurgency in Kashmir. In its aftermath, Kashmir witnessed everyday repercussions of violent conflict—enforced disappearances, the imposition of the controversial Armed Forces (Special Powers) Act (AFSPA), public massacres, and the exodus of the Kashmiri Pandit community. These traumatic events have effectively obscured the city's pre-1947 identity from public consciousness. As if in a trauma response, the place underwent a collective amnesia, losing linkages to its past, at least in public recollections. In the absence of any formal memorialization, the only access Kashmiris have had have to their past is through personal memories and the lifeworlds around them.

÷

Structurally, the book is divided into four chapters. The first chapter, 'It's Pronounced Sirinagar', provides a historical, spatial, cultural, and personal overview of the city. In the successive three chapters, I explore distinct but interconnected lifeworlds in specific geographical stretches of the city. These can be read sequentially or independently. Chapter 2, 'Between Shahr-e-Khas and Downtown', delves into the tension between these two distinct identities of the Old City. Chapter 3, '(Un)Belonging in the Shahr', deals with contesting notions of belonging in newer parts of the city and the 'shahr–gaam' divide, focusing on those who are at the margins of this division. Chapter 4, 'Pale Hands That Love Beside the Shalimar', explores public cultures of leisure in the city, highlighting the complications of Srinagar's identity as a tourist destination. It scrutinizes the impact of conflict and militarization on the everyday lives of people in the city, exploring how it affects their access to leisure and their aspirations for it.

Before we move further, it is important to note that in this account, as would be true of any account of the city, there are some omissions. Some of these are deliberate, driven by logistical constraints and self-censorship, while others are manifestations of my limited knowledge, life experience, and biases inherent in my inclinations and curiosities. As I sat down to write, a lot of questions about disciplinary practice came rushing back to me: should I look at Srinagar as an objective third person? But I could never be objective about it. Should I look at the city through the lens of historians and urban scholars, writers, poets, singers, activists, or human rights scholars? But my context came seeping into the picture—I can only say of the city of what I have seen. I can only reveal those parts of the city that the city decided to reveal to me. Or to be less poetic and more sociological, those parts of the city, which my socio-cultural position as a Muslim Kashmiri woman with certain caste-class privilege and the access that comes with them allows me to.

It is also important to preface this account with the acknowledgment that the story of Kashmir changes as you move away from the city. While Srinagar has often been used as the face of Kashmir by virtue of being the administrative capital, the experiences of those living in Srinagar do not homogeneously reflect the experience of all Kashmiris in the valley. In Kashmir, when we talk about the socio-political struggle that the valley has faced over the past decades, we talk about the valley as a whole and we refrain from using administrative divisions. On the political end, on most critical issues, Kashmir has been able to put out a collective front, one where the internal fault lines don't appear. But the picture that sees the valley as a singular monolithic territory is a dangerous socio-political omission that overlooks the vast array of experiences of Kashmiris living in Kashmir. The violent conflict that has engulfed Kashmir has neither eradicated internal differences in the valley nor has it established uniform lived experiences for all. Instead, it has intertwined with the existing socio-economic divisions, adding heightened complexities and intensifying local experiences of these challenges. I write this book with the awareness that the narratives on Kashmir have been almost entirely Srinagar-centric, and instead of rectifying this scholarly distortion, this book contributes to it. I hope in the future, this unfortunate gap in Kashmir studies is addressed and Kashmiri researchers are presented with opportunities to explore their local contexts.

CHAPTER 1
'IT'S PRONOUNCED SIRINAGAR'

I stood at the gate of the Malkha graveyard, unable to decide if I should enter the cemetery or turn back. My great-grandmother was laid here next to her husband last year; the man had waited a good forty years before our family matriarch decided to join him. Her stepdaughter, my grandmother, along with my grandfather is buried in Pattan, and since my father visits the Pattan graveyard more often to offer fatiha to my grandparents, I am more familiar with that side of the family's deceased and apologetically have not been able to visit this side of my ancestry often. When I started writing this book, I found myself introspecting about my connection with the city. I was inevitably led to this graveyard as the beginning point of my association with Srinagar. I stood there as a researcher, conscious of the keywords that fit the setting, except I felt nothing. I tried to force a sense of connection with my ancestry, but I was a year too late to the funeral and all the mourners had left.

I had no idea how to find her grave, and even though I have always been terrified of graveyards—scared of offending the dead or hearing from them the things they have seen in the afterlife—I moved around trying to locate her. I looked into the distance at the numerous tombstones and bunches of yemberzal flowers sprouting haphazardly. I saw some graves whose tombstones had fallen into oblivion, and others that were covered with fresh rose petals, but there was no sign of her. Looking up, I found before me a magnificent view of Haer Parbat (also known as the Koh-i-Maran), crowned by the Haer Parbat Fort.

Due to its strategic position, the hill provides a clear 360-degree view of the city and the water network snaking through it. As a result, it has always had significant military importance for imperial forces ruling Kashmir, allowing them to track advances on the city. It was on the Haer Parbat that Akbar carried out his first architectural intervention in Kashmir in the sixteenth century, constructing a fortress and fortifying the area around the hill to mark his administrative centre, the city of Nagar Nagar. Later, from the mid-eighteenth century to early nineteenth century, when the Afghans ruled Kashmir, Ata Mohammad Khan Barakzai (r. 1806–13), the longest-serving governor of Kashmir of the Durrani empire, built the fort which currently rests on the hill. Since then, as the rulers changed, so has their insignia on the fort; it passed then to Sikh rule, Dogra rule, and currently, the Indian flag stands hoisted on the fort.

Apart from the political and military significance, this stretch has been the centre of socio-cultural and religious life in Kashmir. Haer Parbat is considered sacred by Kashmiri Pandits. According to Hindu mythology, Haer Parbat was once inhabited by an asura (demon) named Jalodbhava. People prayed to Goddess Parvati for help and succour from the evil presence. She took the form of a bird and dropped a pebble above the asura. As it fell, the small stone grew larger and larger, and finally, it crushed Jalodbhava when it landed on his head. Haer Parbat is revered as that pebble, thereby giving the name Haer, referring to the common myna, and Parbat, the hill. One of the names under which Parvati is worshipped by Kashmiri Pandits is Sharika, and the middle part of the western slope of the hill houses the Sharika Devi Temple (also known as the Shri Chakreshwari Temple), where Parvati is depicted with eighteen arms and sitting in Shri Chakra, a complex sacred geometry. Just outside the Kaeth Darwaza (the main entrance) of Haer Parbat Fort is a gurudwara, Chatti Patshahi, built to commemorate the visit of the sixth Sikh guru, Guru Hargobind Singh, to Kashmir and is a significant place for the Kashmiri Sikh community. To the south of the hill stands the shrine of Hamza Makhdoom, a sixteenth-century Sufi saint. Locally known as Makhdoom Saeb, the place holds immense reverence for Muslims in the valley, and people from different parts of the valley flock to the shrine and offer prayers and niyaz (offerings). I remember racing my siblings up the eighty stone stairs to Makhdoom Saeb's shrine, strategically dodging groups of people offering taher (a traditional turmeric rice dish distributed on

city as memory

joyous occasions and as religious offering), bearded men asking for niyaz, vendors selling toys, and people in need asking for money to reach the top. At the summit, we would run from one vantage point to another, looking at the panoramic view of Srinagar uninterrupted by phone lines and electrical wires while our parents prayed.

The Haer Parbat Fort itself recently opened to the public in 2007 after being closed during the insurgency for nearly twenty years. When I visited the fort for the first time last year, I was stunned by the uninterrupted view of the city that I had been chasing since my childhood; it had been here all along, only made inaccessible by barricades and barbed wires. Wading through the rundown stairways, I reached what looked like observation posts, strategically spread across the fort, and through the old and unkempt windows of the fort, the whole of Srinagar revealed itself, in all its minute details. Through the windows, I could see the overview of the city, where amongst the sprawling urbanization, the architectural motifs on the landscape of the city, the Jamia Masjid complex, Chatti Badshahi Gurudwara, Khanqah-e-Maula, amongst others, stood out. The windows provided a closer view of the water networks that surround Srinagar, and I tried to imagine how the city would have looked a century ago with the Nallah Mar running through the heart of the city, water transportation connecting the parts of the city, and the city to the rest of Kashmir. The one frame of the Haer Parbat that I saw from my great-grandmother's graveyard contained, in each element, a vital fragment of the Srinagar story.

As I stepped outside, my contemplation was broken by a series of successive whistles from a military convey, and I was woken up to the present reality of Srinagar. As the cavalry passed by, several brightly coloured posters with Prime Minister Narendra Modi's face and details of the G20 event peeked at me from the vehicles. Srinagar was hosting the G20 Tourism Working Group meeting under India's G20 presidency in May 2023. Foreign delegates from twenty-seven countries were visiting Srinagar to participate in the meeting. This was the first such official international visit since the abrogation of Article 370 in 2019. Consequently, security was intensified, and the event was heavily publicized to mark 'Kashmir's return to normalcy'.

I walked along the length of the graveyard on the remnants of a footpath to reach the other side. I noticed the far end of the graveyard had enormous structures on both sides; one side was an under-construction multi-floored concrete monstrosity that is supposed to be a nursing school, and on the other side stood a board that read 'Makhdoom Sahib Rope Way by JK Tourism'. The ropeway was accompanied by a building which was decorated with hoardings of different coloured fish; it said 'Kashmir Trout'. I had arrived from Delhi a couple of days earlier, and it had been a while since I had visited this side of the city, so I was still coming to terms with the infrastructural changes as well as the sheer scale of the G20 insignia that had taken over the city.

I stopped to look at the magnificent Haer Parbat one last time, and at the graves that rested peacefully at its foothills, and found myself thinking: in this rapidly urbanizing 'Smart City' of Srinagar, how long would the dead be allowed to rest in this historically and culturally significant landscape, which has been reduced to its potential as lucrative real estate? Once the cable car tourism expands, the nursing home occupies the other half, and the living start encroaching on the little space that was left for the dead, the view of the Haer Parbat will be blocked by a series of banal structures. Will the coming generations be able to forge a sense of connection with visual scapes devoid of their collective historical, cultural, and personal memories?

I drove past the grand G20 billboard advertisements and the new 'smart bunkers' in the strife-torn Smart City of Srinagar. Government officials had commented unironically that the aim behind beautifying the bunkers was to maintain surveillance but with a more aesthetically pleasing appearance. I moved past the newly renovated Polo View market which had been made fancy for the foreign delegates. The tiled stretch of barely 150 metres, meant to be a recreational space in the middle of the city, was guarded by eight police vehicles and close to a dozen fully armed personnel. Moving about Srinagar, I noticed that a lot of new infrastructural additions in the city, like the 'I LOVE Srinagar' signages, Indian flags, and tricoloured lights had been added, perhaps to ensure that there is visual continuity with other Indian cities.

On these hoardings, selfie points, T-shirts, and fridge magnets, 'Srinagar' was spelled the way one saw in newspapers, reports by human rights organizations, and other historical and political accounts. Yet it felt different on these surfaces. It looked brighter, happier than the city I knew Srinagar to be; perhaps it is what airbrushing the context can do to names. I realized the distance I felt at the sight of the term 'Srinagar' was also a product of my auditory experience of hearing the name. The realization came to me a couple of weeks later when I went to meet academic and media trainer, Dr Rashid Maqbool, at the department of media studies at the University of Kashmir. Our first conversation is memorable because, within the first five minutes of our meeting, Dr Rashid stood up suddenly and started to trace Srinagar's historically evolving boundaries on a sheet of paper he put up on the chart board of his office. After a conversation of forty minutes, we finally got to exchanging names and discussing the purpose of my visit, when he politely interjected in Kashmiri, 'Before we move any further, I must point out that you are pronouncing the name wrong. It is not Srinagar, there is no *sri* sound in Kashmiri. It's pronounced *Siri*nagar.'

At that moment, it dawned on me that I had never actually heard anyone in Kashmir, including my own family, friends, relatives, and acquaintances (who did not go to convent schools) say 'Srinagar'. It was always Sirinagar. After years of staying in Delhi and having heard the term being used in mainstream media, academia, popular culture, and airport announcements over and over again, I had internalized the non-Kashmiri pronunciation of the name. Every time I heard it being said as 'Sirinagar', I had been subconsciously correcting the pronunciation in my head. After our meeting, I stood outside Kashmir University for a while, relearning the 'mispronunciation' I had learned to needlessly correct. 'Sirinagar', 'Sirinagar'.

÷

Interestingly, the name Srinagar has not existed in history continuously, but has disappeared in phases, and then reappeared in common usage. The first traces of the name 'Srinagar' have been found in Kalhana's *Rajatarangni*, one of the oldest accounts of the history of Kashmir. According to him, Kashmir had several capitals, the most important of which was the ancient city of Srinagari founded by Buddhist king, Ashoka, in 250 BCE. The remnants of Srinagari, 'the city of Sri', an appellation of Goddess Lakshmi, can be found in the Pandrethan village, which falls under the present-day Badami Bagh army cantonment located on the outskirts of Srinagar. After the middle of the sixth century CE, it was replaced by a city called Pravarapura, named after its founder Pravarasen II, which is said to have been located near the Haer Parbat hillock. Since this newly founded city existed in close proximity to the older city, people continued using the old name. As a result, Pravarapura never caught on, and Srinagari continued to be used to refer to the capital city of Kashmir.

Successive rulers moved their capitals to other cities in the valley, prominent amongst which are Parishaspurha (present-day Parihaspor) founded by Lalitaditya in eighth century CE, Jayapura (present-day Anderkot) founded by Lalitaditya's great-grandson, Jayapida, in an attempt to compete with his grandfather's popularity in the later part of the eighth century, and Avantipura (present-day Auntpur) founded by Avantivarman in ninth century CE. However, these cities did not to stand the test of time and disintegrated, and even as the use of Srinagari was discontinued, the capital was moved back territorially to that area.

From 1320 to 1819, during the Muslim rule of Kashmir, the city was referred to as 'Kashmir', identical to the name of the region itself, rather than 'Srinagar'. This period encompasses the Sultanate era founded by Rinchan Shah, a Ladakhi noble who converted to Islam, the Shah Mir dynasty (1339–1561), the Chak dynasty (1561–1589), as well as the Mughal rule. Various Muslim rulers showed preferences for specific parts of the city, and their historical influences can still be traced in some areas today. Rinchan Shah (r. 1320–23), the first Muslim ruler, established Rinchanpura, roughly situated around today's Aael Kadal. Alauddin (r. 1344–56) founded Alauddinpura, nestled between the present-day Jamia Masjid and Aael Kadal. Shihabuddin (r. 1354–73) chose the area around the Haer Parbat as his capital, while Zain-ul-Abidin (r. 1420–70) established Naushahr, known today as Nowshahr. Sultan Haidar Shah (r. 1470–72) shifted the capital to Navyut, but it returned to Naushahr from 1472–84. It is important to note that in the line of rulers, Zain-ul-Abidin, affectionately known as Budshah (the Great King), stands out for his influence on Srinagar. He reigned over Kashmir from 1418 to 1419 and then from 1420 to 1470, and is remembered as one of its most progressive rulers. He championed religious tolerance, revoking the jizya tax on non-Muslims and promoting the study of Sanskrit, translating Sanskrit works into Persian. As an arts patron, he invited expert craftsmen from other countries, especially Samarkand, to train his subjects. Kashmir's most cherished handicrafts, including carpet weaving, embroidery, silver and copperware, papier mâché, woodwork carving, khatamband (traditional Kashmiri woodwork ceiling design made by combining wooden slats of walnut, deodar, or fir into interlocking polygonal patterns), and pashmina shawls were introduced during his time. He encouraged educational and cultural exchanges, his reign witnessing several scholars and artisans from different regions, especially Central Asia, coming to Kashmir and teaching their craft to the local population. Many communities engaged in handicrafts still reside across the city in occupation-based localities, preserving and practising their crafts using techniques passed down since Budshah's reign.

During the subsequent Mughal rule, the term 'Srinagar' continued to remain in disuse. Most Mughal chroniclers referred to the city simply as 'Kashmir' or 'Shahr-e-Kashmir'. Yet, within Shahr-e-Kashmir, the Mughals created a distinct city—Nagar Nagar. Kashmir was a part of the Mughal empire from the end of the sixteenth century to the early eighteenth century, for a total of 166 years. The Mughal empire's attempts to invade and control Kashmir's territory started with Babur (r. 1526–30), continued with Humayun (r. 1530–40; 1555–56), and were finally realized during Akbar's (r. 1556–1605) rule in 1589, which marked the end of independent Muslim rule in the valley with the downfall of the Chak dynasty. The Mughal invasion of Kashmir initially met some opposition. However, over the course of time, the local population became more accepting of the regime. This is largely due to the regime's attentive administrative set-up and stable governing policies. The project of Kashmir held special significance for the Mughals who saw the valley as an idealized garden and sought to recreate gardens similar to the ones in their homelands of Persia and Central Asia; it is for this reason that the present-day Mughal gardens have the most visible influences of the Islamic gardens of Persian tradition. Traveller François Bernier writes, 'It is not indeed without reason that the *Mogols* call *Kachemire* the terrestrial paradise of the Indies, or that *Ekbar* was so unremitting in his efforts to wrest the sceptre from the hand of its native Princes', referring to

Akbar's annexation of Kashmir through the disposition and exile of Yusuf Shah Chak, the fourth sultan of the Chak dynasty and the last independent Muslim ruler of the Kashmir valley who was invited to Delhi on the pretexts of talks with the Mughal regime but deceitfully imprisoned and exiled in Bihar. The literal and metaphorical implications of this act are captured by Basharat Peer in his book *Curfewed Nights* where he says, 'Yusuf Shah's imprisonment and betrayal by Akbar has become a metaphor for the relationship between Delhi and Srinagar…. After Yusuf Shah Chak, Kashmir was never free.'

Zareef Ahmad Zareef, a prominent Kashmiri poet and writer born in 1943, has closely observed the evolution of Srinagar. He often discusses the Kashmiri relationship with the Mughals. Due to the oppressive policies of the Chak dynasty against Sunnis, Kashmiris sought Mughal intervention. Consequently, when Akbar invaded Kashmir on 5 June 1589, he assured the Kashmiris several rights. Among the promises were religious freedom, recognition of Kashmiris as free individuals, the involvement of the Chak family in administration, and the abolition of certain taxes and customs. However, these gestures of goodwill did not stop the Mughals from exerting their military might on Kashmir and plundering local resources. Akbar also prohibited Kashmiris from bearing arms or joining the military, limiting their ability to provide any resistance to Mughal rule.

Akbar seized Kashmir's treasures from the state's reserves, which included gold, jewels, silver, shahtoosh, and pashmina shawls. Zareef Ahmad Zareef notes that in protest, Kashmiris locked their homes, took to the rooftops, and chanted slogans like 'Sonas rupas karun dagul, maghul logum balaiye (Took away our treasured gold and silver, Mughals brought travesty with them)' and 'Shikas mogoul sund buoul khudyan gol; poge mogoul sund buel khudayan gol (The seed of the miserable Mughal, may God perish it; the seed of destroyer Mughal, may God perish it)'. With the Mughals settling in, their soldiers sprawled all around the city and their presence was resented by the local population, who were subjected to frequent harassment. Acknowledging this, Akbar ordered his soldiers to remain within the confines of the walled city of Nagar Nagar on the Haer Parbat, situated away from the indigenous population of the city. Characterized by its Mughal grandeur, whitewashed buildings, and ornate decorations, Nagar Nagar stood in stark contrast to the original capital, which was marred by neglect and repeated incidents of fire.

Although Mughal rule was not fully embraced by Kashmiris, their aesthetic contributions have left a lasting mark on the cultural and ecological landscape of Kashmir. They introduced notable architectural designs and cultivated gardens, with a particular emphasis on valuing and preserving the indigenous chinar trees. Among the numerous Mughal structures in the valley,

city as memory

only the series of gardens known as the Mughal Gardens, the Pathar Masjid constructed by Empress Nur Jahan in 1623, and the Mullah Shah Complex erected by Dara Shikoh in 1649 have predominantly survived. Interestingly, the Mughal mosques never became popular as is evident from the fact that neither Pathar Masjid (also called Naev Masheed) nor the Mullah Shah Mosque have been used for prayers by the locals. One of the theories proposed to explain the absence of worshippers in the former is attributed to an anecdote involving Nur Jahan. It is said that when she was asked about the cost of building the mosque, she pointed to her shoe, implying that it cost her very little. Consequently, many scholars during her time and later discouraged praying there. However, rejection of the Pathar Masjid may stem from several factors. These include the use of white limestone as a building material in a cold region where wood is more commonly used, the building's architectural deviation from traditional Kashmiri styles (the pyramidal roof seen in most mosques is absent), and the perception of the Mughals as foreign rulers not aligned with indigenous customs and sentiments.

The end of Muslim rule in Kashmir came in 1819 with the annexation of Afghans by the Sikhs under the leadership of Maharaja Ranjit Singh (r. 1801–39). This marked the culmination of five centuries of Muslim governance—a watershed moment for both its Hindu and Muslim inhabitants. It was during the revivalist spree of the Sikh rule in 1819 that the ancient Hindu name of the city was revived. From that point onwards, the name has been commonly used, albeit with a deviation in the local vernacular, making it 'Sirinagar'.

÷

The story of Srinagar has been punctuated by formidable adversities, brought about by both natural disasters and man-made catastrophes. The notions of stability for the inhabitants have been shaken by a series of large-scale natural disasters like floods, earthquakes, and famines. In the latter half of the nineteenth century, cholera epidemics, famines, and fires ravaged populations in the city. By the twentieth century, the city continued to grapple with imperialist forces that viewed Kashmir merely as a territory to be romanticized, occupied, and then commercialized as a retreat or for revenue, often disregarding the needs and interests of the local population.

Throughout medieval times, especially between the sixteenth and eighteenth centuries, the city had to face the wrath of severe famines, some induced by floods, others by unpredictable weather conditions and inadequate storage facilities. The floods of 1640–42 were so catastrophic that they obliterated 438 Kashmiri villages, leaving nothing behind—not even the names of the villages survived. The famine of 1745–46 is said to have wiped off 38 per cent of the valley's population, leaving the city of Srinagar with just around 200,000 inhabitants. The famine is said to have forced one-third of the valley's population to cross the mountain pass to Punjab. Successive famines inspired the Kashmiri proverb 'Drag tsalih ta dag tsalih na (the famine goes but its stains remain)', which is still invoked with a spine-chilling dread. The indigenous population, already oppressed under the self-serving rule of foreign powers like the Mughals and Afghans, was further devastated by periodic earthquakes and floods that destroyed lives and livelihoods on a massive scale. Even though the Mughals are said to have made some efforts for relief, they were grossly inadequate compared to the scale of the calamities.

As Srinagar plodded towards modernity, owing to the neglect of the Afghan, Sikh, and early Dogra rulers to the basic infrastructure of the city, it was severely underprepared to meet the challenges of modern times. Primarily constructed from wood, the city was inherently susceptible to fires, and in the absence of any city planning measures, the situation was made more dangerous due to the close and haphazard way in which the buildings were constructed. The road system in Kashmir was not built till the British Residency intervened in 1882, and in the absence of roads, there were no suitable measures to contain fires. As a result, even controllable fires would end up ravaging parts of the city. During the reign of Maharaja Ranbir Singh (r. 1856–85), a significant portion of Srinagar was consumed by fire, and before he ascended the throne, the city had been burnt down sixteen times. Poor city planning and unsanitary health conditions had made Srinagar a hub of cholera outbreaks.

Apart from the obvious physical and psychological damage owing to these catastrophic events, Srinagar's cultural sphere was rendered unstable by the changing ideological beliefs and priorities of its foreign rulers. After prolonged Mughal control, the city fell into unstable hands at the beginning of the Afghan rule. All in a matter of 150 years, Kashmir had witnessed the quick emergence and consequent toppling of the Afghan, Sikh, and Dogra rule.

Capturing the impact of this instability on the psychological and social fabric of Kashmir, Walter R. Lawrence observed:

> The dependence on the whims and idiosyncrasies of foreigners of brief authority, coupled with the fact that the Kashmiris never knew how long the rule from which these strange governors drew their power would last, has had a powerful influence on the character of the people, and there is strong and hereditary disbelief in the permanence of institutions and in the benevolence of rulers. Perhaps no country furnishes so curious a record of constant change as Kashmir, and it is a matter of surprise that under the rapid transition of governments, varying in race, religion, and language, the people of the valley should have retained their peculiar nationality unimpaired.

city as memory

Each of the rulers entered the territory with their imperialist agendas and visions for the land and the local population was forced to comply, and out of these rulers, some were more radical than others. The Afghans came to Kashmir in 1753 and ruled for sixty-six years, bringing with them a radical interpretation of Sunni Islam and a complete disregard for Kashmir's socio-cultural dynamics. Their rule is remembered for large-scale official oppression, squandering of state resources, a decline in agricultural output, significant depletion of wealth due to excessive taxation (including the imposition of dag shawl, an excise tax on shawls which further exacerbated the condition of weavers), poor governance, political turmoil, and a penchant for elite and aristocratic luxuries. They not only displayed a complete lack of interest in public welfare but also harboured resentment towards previous cultural and infrastructural contributions by the Mughals, such as their gardens and the city of Nagar Nagar. Their reign saw brutal and mass persecution of Kashmiri Shia Muslims, Pandits, and other religious minorities, and revival of the jizya tax on Hindus. Affluent Sunni Muslims were also not spared and any form of dissent was met with disproportional brutality. Capturing the political and cultural shock that Kashmir witnessed in the shift from Mughal to Afghan rule, a poet wrote:

> Pursidam az kharabiye gulshan zi baghban
> Afghan kashid guft ki Afghan kharab kard.
>
> (I enquired of the gardener the cause of the destruction of the garden.
> Drawing a deep sigh he replied, 'It is the Afghans who did it.')

The Sikh regime replaced Afghan rule in 1819. While their rule lasted for only twenty-seven years, it marked the end of five centuries of Muslim reign in Kashmir. During this time, the trajectory of Kashmir's socio-economic progress continued to decline steadily due to neglect of public welfare, city planning, and sanitation, which was exacerbated by years of famine, cholera, and plague. Thousands perished, while thousands more fled the valley. It is estimated that the population of Kashmir plummeted from 800,000 to 200,000 by the 1840s. An implication of this change in the political regime was that the state sympathies shifted in favour of Kashmiri Sikhs and Pandits and resulted in large-scale execution of Kashmiri Muslims. Reflecting on the harsh treatment of Muslims by Sikh officials, P. N. K Bamzai notes how Sikh militancy and civil officials were used to strong opposition from Muslims in the Punjab and frontier districts and adopted a very aggressive stance to it. They continued to use the same strategies against Kashmiri Muslims, notwithstanding the decades of impoverishment and exploitation the

city as memory

majority population had faced at the hands of Afghans. Sameer Hamdani, historian and design director at the Indian National Trust for Art and Cultural Heritage (INTACH), Kashmir, says that the agenda of the Sikh rule was largely concerned 'with rectifying past Muslim "excesses" against the Kashmiri Hindus'. As the communal nature of the court changed in favour of Kashmiri Hindus, the Sikh rulers tried to enforce large-scale changes on the religious and cultural front. These included shutting down the Jamia Masjid in Srinagar, forbidding the azaan, banning beef consumption, and making the killing of cows a capital punishment for which the offenders were publicly executed. The Sikh rule is also notorious for its imposition of heavy taxation, which further exacerbated the conditions of impoverished cultivators and traders, many of whom left Kashmir in large numbers. While Kashmiri shawls were receiving acclaim globally, the taxation policies implemented by the Sikhs caused significant distress to the local artisans.

Sikh rule in Kashmir concluded in 1846 with the signing of the Treaty of Amritsar between the British government and Maharaja Gulab Singh (r. 1822–46), founder of the Dogra dynasty and subsequently the first maharaja of the princely state of Jammu and Kashmir. During the first Anglo-Sikh War in 1846, Gulab Singh collaborated with the British, undermining the Sikh Army and aiding a British victory. In recognition of his services, the British agreed to transfer the territory they had acquired from the Sikhs to Gulab Singh. As a result, Kashmir was ceded to him for 7.5 million nanakshahee rupees (approximately ₹7,500,000), and he was conferred the title of maharaja of the princely state of Kashmir. This marked the beginning of Dogra rule, and it was during this time that Srinagar started taking steady steps towards modernization. As the British Residency established its foothold in Kashmir, they pushed for Srinagar's urban development, as a result of which the city started receiving infrastructural and administrative facelifts. In 1890, the Jhelum Valley Cart Road was constructed, improving Srinagar's connectivity with the rest of India, ending its prolonged geographical seclusion. This improved accessibility, combined with British interest in the valley, led to the revival of Kashmir, and Srinagar in particular, as a tourist spot. European officials, eager to escape the stifling heat of the plains and seeking landscapes similar to England, began to view the region as both a health retreat and a leisure destination.

While the primary motivation for Srinagar's urban development included making the city palatable to European residents and visitors, these undertakings inadvertently set the stage for Srinagar's subsequent urban growth. During the reign of Maharaja Pratap Singh (r. 1885–1925), the city witnessed progress in education and public services. It marked the establishment of Sri Pratap College, Srinagar's first institution affiliated with Punjab University, along with many high schools and hospitals. Sericulture, transport, tourism, and various other industries developed in Srinagar, generating employment and attracting people from different areas of Kashmir to the city. Administrative domains like the forest department, customs, and excise witnessed comprehensive overhauls. Additionally, in 1886, the groundwork for municipal administration was set in place, which played a vital role in sanitizing the city and reducing the number of cholera epidemics in Srinagar.

Despite progressive steps, the Dogra court largely upheld its communal disposition, reflected in its governing policies. The period was characterized by increasingly harsh taxation measures, which disproportionately burdened local traders, cultivators, and peasants, the majority of whom were Muslims. Elucidating their impact on the Shawl trade, G. M. D. Sufi writes:

> Wool was taxed as it entered Kashmir. The manufacturer was taxed for every workman he employed and also at various stages of the process according to the value of the fabric. Lastly, there was the enormous duty of 85 per cent *ad valorem*. Butchers, bakers, carpenters, boatmen, and even prostitutes were taxed. Poor coolies, who were engaged to carry loads for travellers had to give up half their earnings.

Such oppressive anti-worker policies led to resentment against the Dogra regime. One of the earliest public expressions against Dogra rulers was led by the shawl weavers in 1865 who agitated to improve their working conditions. The revolt was brutally suppressed, the extent of which can be measured by the fact that within three decades, the number of shawl weavers decreased from 28,000 to 5,000. By the 1930s, public discontentment against Dogra rule was palpable, occasionally surfacing as isolated protests. This was complemented by underground political activities spearheaded by the Reading Room Party, which consisted of left-wing Muslim intellectuals that sought to drive the political mobilization against Dogra rule. Tensions reached a tipping point on 13 July 1931, when a large mob sought to breach the Srinagar Jail during the sedition trial of a young man named Abdul Qadeer. The state's heavy-handed response resulted in twenty-two protesters being killed on the spot by the police. The incident and subsequent reaction were viewed as a validation of the resistance against Dogra rule. This local political mobilization was a watershed movement in Kashmir's political landscape, setting the precedent for future cultures of public dissent and resistance.

As these internal events were unfolding in Kashmir, larger political shifts, particularly the Partition of India, added a new layer of complexity to the indigenous struggle against Dogra authority. The valley found itself conditionally acceded to the newly formed state of India, with the promise of a future plebiscite that would let the people choose their political future. The accession led to a recalibration of the resistance movement, shifting its anti-Dogra focus and demands for emancipation from Dogra rule to an assertive vocalization of the overarching quest for territorial integrity. Consequently, India and Pakistan were embroiled in three major wars over Kashmir's territory—in 1947, 1965, and 1999—and Kashmir witnessed an unprecedented local militant uprising over the legitimacy of this merger and the unfulfilled promise of the plebiscite.

After 1947, various attempts were made to infiltrate Kashmir to fuel unrest at a local level, but none of the attempts materialized into mass mobilization. In 1965, under Project Gibraltar, state-backed insurgents from Pakistan infiltrated the valley, carrying with them ammunition and ambitious plans to stir a revolt in Kashmir. The operation did not find any active takers in Kashmir, and this lukewarm reception along with poor planning and weak execution led to the failure of these plans. Between the period from 1947 to 1989, Kashmir witnessed many attempts at politically consolidating the demand for territorial and political sovereignty but none of them had translated into a consolidated movement like in 1989. The escalations that happened from 1989 onwards fully transformed and left behind a foreboding roadmap for future events. Within the span of roughly two years, a full-blown armed revolt which had mass support from the local population broke out in the valley. Arms and trained militants from Pakistan started making the rounds across localities, urging young women and men to support them in flesh and blood. The period also saw Kashmir's largest minority, more than 200,000 Kashmiri Pandits, being forced into an exodus. Large-scale protests and demonstrations erupted across the valley. This was followed by a spectacular rise in the pro-freedom sentiment among the masses and an unprecedented number of civilian deaths, disappearances, and incidents of alleged torture by security forces using AFSPA.

As the bloody events were unfolding, a whole set of words were getting engraved on the bodies and vernacular of Kashmiris: naareh (slogans), tehreek (local reference to armed insurgency in 1989), juloos (procession), AFSPA, CASO (cordon and search operation), crackdown (an impromptu siege announced by the armed forces, wherein male members of households were instructed to assemble in local playgrounds, school compounds, etc., while women and children remained at home, and the armed forces conducted search raids), exodus, migrant camps, mukhbir (police informer), and ikhwan (pro-government militia composed of surrendered Kashmiri militants from the insurgency). The scale of violence that played out in the valley first shocked, and then benumbed all—those who were in the valley and those who had been forced out of it.

Numerous international and local events have been pinpointed by scholars as catalysts for the armed uprising in Kashmir. On the international front, events such as the end of the Cold War, the Soviet withdrawal from Afghanistan, the subsequent rise of the Taliban, and the global surge in Islamist movements significantly influenced regional dynamics. Domestically, the vast mobilization around a pro-freedom narrative, primarily on ethno-religious grounds, was significant. Additionally, the political void left by Sheikh Abdullah's demise, coupled with accusations of the 1987 state elections being rigged by the Indian government in favour of pro-India regional factions intensified public distrust in conventional political processes, paving the way for the armed rebellion. In the collective memory, however, the insurgency movement is remembered as a 'spontaneous revolt'. During the course of writing this book, I spoke to numerous people about their memories of the tehreek, and almost everyone who has a living memory of the uprising emphasized how unexpected the turn of events had been and that no one in their wildest dreams had predicted escalation on such a massive scale.

My father, who had spent the early years of his youth loitering in the streets of Srinagar till the middle of the night in the 80s, found himself locking all the doors and windows of his house by 6 p.m. and developing a strong paranoia of the nebar (outside) within a year. I also met Vivek Raina, the chief executive officer of a Delhi-based broadband company, at his office in Delhi. Vivek's family had migrated out of Srinagar during the mass exodus. As he spoke of his associations with the city, he still recounted with bafflement the suddenness of what had happened—in May 1989, his father was selecting windows for his dream house in Chattbal, Srinagar; by June 1990, they found themselves in a migrant camp in Jammu. Similarly, Neerja Mattoo, former professor at the Women's College, recalled how the college had received an ultimatum in 1989 dictating that all Muslim women cover themselves in an abaya and all Hindu women identify themselves through a bindi. They had all laughed at the ridiculous proposition and torn the letter into pieces. A year later, most students and staff were covered in abayas. Journalist Saima Shakeel's family has been involved in the houseboat tourism business for generations. In 1989, they were busy preparing for the arrival of foreign tourists who would register to stay in their houseboats for a couple of weeks. Suddenly, they found the Dal Lake deserted and the tourism sector crumbling. In just one year, the number of tourist arrivals had dropped by 98 per cent in the valley. Parallelly, the new generation that was being born found a choking reality of violence and suppression as their introduction to life in Kashmir. Born at the peak of turbulence in the 1990s, Muhammad Faysal could not make sense of the fact that despite having belonged to Old City Srinagar for generations, he could not move from one part of the city to another without showing his identity card to men in uniform who had abruptly appeared in his city.

Srinagar unfolded for me through these people and

city as memory

the access they allowed me into their lifeworlds. As we spoke, Srinagar changed forms, morphing out of the mould of the city that has been a passive recipient of macro-historical and political events into a living breathing organism that *is* shaping and *being* shaped by the lives, outlooks, aspirations, and experiences of all those who live within and around it. However, as I navigated from one story to the other, I could tangibly feel the gaps that were left behind. These gaps interwove to create an alternative map of the city, one that was inaccessible to me. There were stories I couldn't stop for, stories I deliberately overlooked, yet some of these stories found their way to me. A young boy who often played cricket in the Eidgah found his cricket team disappearing, some buried in the corner of the Eidgah and others in jails of faraway Indian cities that he couldn't even spot on the map. A young man, sent to work under a senior papier mâché craftsman, found his hands shaking every time he tried to paint the surface of the papier mâché mould that the sakhtasaz artisan had made for him. The silence between successive sounds of bullets and tear gas canisters being fired was not a long enough pause for his hands to regain their steadiness. A middle-aged woman who studied in the stillness of the night while her children slept next to her. Houses with their lamps alight in the dark could be perceived as suspicious by both armed forces and militants, and either group could come knocking on her door. So, she could cover her windows with thick blankets to prevent the light from leaving their room. Some accounts that came to me weren't as sombre. I came across the story of a young boy who journeyed all the way from Srinagar to Varmul, only to stand outside his girlfriend's house, yearning for a mere glimpse. Unable to call or text due to the communication blackout of 2019, he had decided to visit in the hope of seeing her. After a few futile visits, he finally managed to see her. With phones out of service, they ingeniously exchanged love notes via their Bluetooth applications, while she discreetly observed him from her window, and he gazed at her silhouette. I heard stories of two school best friends who lived at a considerable distance and would walk amid curfews to their private tutor's house. They would then proceed to skip classes just to spend some time away from home and with each other. Since phones didn't work, there was no way for their families to find out. These lifeworlds came to me as anecdotes, as stories someone had heard somewhere. They acted as prompts, revealing versions of the city that could look drastically different from what I was looking at in Srinagar. The fact that countless such lifeworlds exist and that the narrative can change dramatically when the dice is flipped was an unsettling realization. Yet, during the process of writing this book, I learned to make peace with it. The regret of not delving deeper into these stories was mitigated by the responsibility I felt towards those who had granted me their time and access to their worlds.

city as memory

My childhood during the mid-90s was when the insurgency movement was on the decline and Kashmir was getting increasingly militarized, and my adolescence in the early 2000s was when Kashmir was undergoing deadly cycles of violence in civilian protests. The thread of political conflict is interwoven with my memories of home, and it is impossible to detangle such macro events from the core memories of the homeland. *Love:* I was a year old when there was a crackdown in my father's ancestral village. New to the intensity of emotions that parenthood invokes, Abu hid me in his pheran and ran off to the nearby village, leaving behind my befuddled mother and enraged grandparents; *fear:* I was on a bus and an armed soldier stopped the vehicle, asked people to get off, and walk to the military check post. Children were asked to sit inside. So, I peeked out to locate my father's pheran in the seemingly endless line of pheran-clad men. I finally understood the English metaphor 'heart in my mouth', and I didn't like it one bit; *disgust*: I stood in front of the TV as the local presenter read out names of the people who had died in the firing at a civilian protest. I kept checking the names of young boys to see if I recognized any of them. Thankfully, no one I knew. *I said thankfully.* I have heard so many versions of these stories that now I am unsure if I was actually even there, or if I experienced these moments through other people's narrations. *Did this actually happen to me or did my brain personalize someone else's story and store it as my experience?*

However, after a while, I found this self-doubt irrelevant, I was a witness to these memories, some personal and some collective.

I see Srinagar as an extension of this feeling, as a repository of memories: some my own and some shared. As I said before, I never meant for this to be an objective account of the city. It is an exploration into the various associations that people have with the city and with the memory of Srinagar. Each of the lifeworlds explored gives an idea of what Srinagar looks like from a unique vantage point, and out of all the possible associations, what points in history, which political events, and which personal inclinations have become the formative basis of the bond with the city as whole, and what do these choices tell us about the essence and character of Sirinagar.

CHAPTER 2

BETWEEN SHAHR-E-KHAS AND DOWNTOWN

It was the winter of 1985. A brand new black Yezdi CL2 dashed out of Khanna Motors in Safa Kadal onto the Srinagar–Baramulla National Highway. With the chilly December wind in his hair, a young man traversed the narrow lanes of his matamaal in Jamia Kadeem in Downtown. He moved onto the vast stretches of the Boulevard Road, whizzing past the markets of Lal Chowk and the crowded Batmalyun bus stop, delving into the infinite vastness that the highway tends to become. My father drove past the stunned faces of my grandparents who couldn't fathom for the life of them why their son, barely a couple of years into government service, had purchased a motorcycle that cost twenty times his salary. My father was unfazed, for he had found the means to stretch the limits of his freedom. Suddenly, everything was reachable, surmountable.

In my imagination, Downtown Srinagar/Old City/Shahr-e-Khas is forever linked to my father's youth and the filtered adventures he has chosen to share with me. However, I have always suspected that a lot is censored in his retellings of the past that would spontaneously start every time we were visiting Srinagar from Varmul.

As soon as we took the first left towards the Cement Bridge from Qamarwor, my father would assume the role of a city guide and a storyteller. Pointing at anything and everything that seemed significant for his stories or for our general knowledge of the city, he would start naming and contextualizing the place for us. As disinterested teenagers, me and my siblings did not appreciate these guided tours. We would quickly plug back our earphones at the briefest pause between his stories. But this was only possible as long as we moved along the newer parts of the city; the minute we passed through the Baab Dyambaem gate and entered the Old City, the stories would progressively multiply, the beginning of one overlapping with the ending of the other. My wavering attention span allowed me to listen to these stories at different points of their progression, and by the end of our journey, I would carry in my head a mass of someone else's memories that all took place in this tiny, hyperactive, congested place called Downtown.

Abu left Srinagar in 1987 when his position in the survey and investigation division of the Jammu and Kashmir Irrigation and Flood Control Department became permanent. He was transferred to Varmul, where he eventually decided to settle down after a couple of years. When my father moved cities, the signs of insurgency and its violent aftermath had not fully unfolded in Kashmir yet. He experienced that phase of our political history in Varmul, so he has

city as memory

been able to create a temporal pause in his memories of Srinagar. When he comes back to the city, he comes back to the nostalgia of his youth, choosing to overlook most temporal and spatial markers of change. Till date, whenever we visit Srinagar with him, he still points out at every other corner to recount familiar incidents. That time he drove to Boher Kadal at 2 a.m. because his friend's child was craving a kulfi. When he walked to Jamia Kadeem from Palladium Cinema at 1 a.m. because there was no mode of transport. When he and his friends went together to get the hippie hairstyle and his grandfather was horrified by it. Where he stayed when he ran away from his matamaal. His first office building. His first rented accommodation in Naw Kadal. The stories of his youth made my father seem like someone else, someone who could have been him. Even as now the roads he drives through are all widened, standardized, and transformed, he uses his memory to constrict them and recreate the city of his nostalgia.

In 1997, a decade after Abu had left the city, the same roads and lanes that had presented my father with the gift of carefree mobility offered a very different spatial and emotional experience to a young boy who found himself in Naw Kadal after being deboarded from a bus going from Rainwoar to Lal Bazar. This was the first time eight-year-old Muhammad Faysal had been in a crackdown alone. He, along with his co-passengers, was made to stand in a queue with around 150–200 people, all waiting for their talashi (search). As he was waiting for his turn to be frisked, a massive poster of Maqbool Bhat, separatist leader and founder of Jammu Kashmir Liberation Front (JKLF), caught his eye. He fidgeted nervously, sticking his head out to see the faces in front of him and the endless line of people behind him. As the queue moved slowly with army men frisking those before him, a fear that had slowly started to build up suddenly gripped him. He feared if the army men found out he was a Kashmiri and that too from Downtown, they would kill him. When the army man came forward to frisk him, his pounding heart made a feeble attempt to save him. He looked at the army man and in a pretend accent said, 'Main yahan sey nahi hu, mai Dilli sey hu (I am not from here, I am from Delhi).' The army man looked at his visibly Kashmiri nose in a sea of Kashmiri faces, all waiting to be frisked in the centre of Downtown. He smirked and signalled Faysal to leave. In a matter of ten years, things in the city had changed so drastically that even children who understood nothing of the political conflict around them understood the burden of carrying the Kashmiri identity, even while growing up in the heart of Kashmir. The insurgency, which erupted in 1989, finds its roots deeply embedded in the historical dispute over Kashmir's local autonomy and the unresolved question of plebiscite promised to it in the Instrument of Accession. After Kashmir's conditional integration with India in 1947, democratic

city as memory

processes remained hampered in the valley until the 1970s. By 1988, many democratic reforms initiated by the government were rolled back, fostering widespread discontent and public mistrust regarding the intentions of creating a free democracy in Kashmir. The tipping point occurred in 1987, when new elections were conducted only four months after the swearing-in of the chief minister, Farooq Abdullah. Along with the Jammu and Kashmir National Conference and the Indian National Congress, the Muslim United Front (MUF), a coalition of Islamic parties, also contested the elections. The results were reportedly rigged to prevent the central government from losing control of the state's politics. Feeling disenfranchized and disillusioned with the democratic avenues, some MUF leaders turned to armed violence against the state. The rigged elections were seen as a symbol of discarding the public mandate and are widely considered a significant point when protests, strikes, and attacks on Indian government forces intensified, signalling the beginning of the insurgency in earnest.

Notably, from the 1940s to the late 1970s, differences over political ideologies marked specific pockets in Srinagar. Of the two ideological factions, the Sher (Lion) and the Bakra (Goat), Downtown was seen as the stronghold of the latter. The term 'Sher' was derived from Sheikh Muhammad Abdullah's moniker, Sher-e-Kashmir (Lion of Kashmir), while 'Bakra' referred to the beards worn by Islamic clerics, symbolizing piety. The Sher faction aligned with the National Conference, advocating for maximum autonomy for Kashmir within India. Conversely, the Bakras, followers of Mirwaiz Mohammad Farooq and the Awami Action Committee, envisioned Kashmir's future with Pakistan. This ideological schism often fuelled heated debates, and occasionally escalated into physical altercations, both over local issues and Kashmir's broader political future. However, by 1983, the fervour of the Sher–Bakra divide began to wane with the onset of insurgency.

The conflict in Kashmir intensified after 1989, resulting in a political and humanitarian disaster. Thousands were killed, and many more were injured; livelihoods were lost and homes destroyed. Many vanished as 'enforced disappearances'. The Kashmiri Pandit community, the largest religious minority in the valley, was forced into an exodus. Additionally, the insurgency had a profound impact on the psychological, economic, and social aspects of life in the state, severely hampering them. Existence was reduced to 'bare life', a term used by Italian Philosopher, Giorgio Agamben to describe a condition in which individuals are reduced to their mere biological existence, stripped of any legal or social protections.

Downtown, like the rest of Kashmir, was completely transformed by the jolting political and socio-cultural changes that took place in the valley within a mere few years from 1989, leaving those who had seen normalcy in a state of crippling disbelief and ensnaring the coming generations in lifelong trauma about their humanity and political existence.

÷

To understand the scale of conflict and understand its impact on the lives of Kashmiris, Downtown Srinagar emerges as the obvious ground zero. Everything started from there. The first show of the gun in public, the proclamation of Kashmir's revolt through the tehreek, the establishment of the separatist leadership, the crumbling of state order, the euphoric crowds waiting for azaadi to arrive, and the coffins of protestors for whom death arrived at point-blank ranges on the path to freedom—all unfolded in the streets of Downtown. The period that marked the build-up and peak of the insurgency movement in Kashmir is remembered as one of mass euphoria in collective memory, and the streets of Downtown are replete with accounts of that brief phase of ecstasy. In the earlier years, marches of celebrations and protests were held across the city. People came with decorative buntings, some burst crackers, and some distributed baadam mithae amongst the crowds. Experts attribute this mass euphoria to a string of significant geopolitical events, including the Soviet withdrawal from Afghanistan, the fall of the Berlin Wall, and the reunification of Germany. In each of these events, public mobilization against imperialist powers were considered to be crucial for their success. Emboldened by these global milestones, the idea of freedom seemed within reach, and people prepared themselves to receive 'phoolon wali azaadi (the glorious freedom)', as it was highly rumoured to arrive in a matter of days. Even within this euphoric trance, it remained unclear what azaadi meant for different people. For some, it was self-determination; for some, it was a merger with Pakistan; and for some, it meant freedom from Indian rule. Nevertheless, people waited for it. In some areas, people had started symbolically burning Indian currency to mark the end of old systems and indicate the arrival of new ones. In other areas, people had stopped stocking up on food to make space for produce from the other side of the border. Downtown had, supposedly, zones of independence which were safe zones for local and foreign militants to hide. Militants trained in Pakistan and different locations in Kashmir would make appearances at public processions, chant anti-state and pro-freedom slogans, flash their Kalashnikovs, and receive heroic welcomes. The movement reached its pinnacle in 1989, during the kidnapping of Rubaiya Sayeed, the daughter of the then union home minister, Mufti Mohammad Sayeed, and the subsequent release of the militants from the JKLF by the state. Founded in 1976, the JKLF was a militant separatist organization that was active until 1996. Operating as an armed political separatist group in both the Indian- and Pakistani-administered territories of Kashmir, JKLF engaged in various violent activities, including throwing bombs, organizing kidnappings, and conducting targeted killings, particularly during the insurgency years of 1989 and 1990. As the state government under National Conference and the central government under the National Front coalition, comprising the Janata Dal party, Bharatiya Janata Party (BJP), and the Left Front, yielded to pressure, the militancy movement received a boost. Even those in the valley who had been sceptical of the impact of the resistance movement were impressed as they watched the state apparatus crumble.

The momentum gained by the movement in its initial years was swiftly countered by the state's aggressive retaliation. As weapons freely circulated in the market, new militant groups frequently sprang up, each with its own definition of freedom and set of guidelines for civilians to follow. The entry of state-backed Ikhwanis, pro-government militias, added another layer of complexity to the indigenous militancy movement. By 1995, the movement had started showing signs of waning, partly due to the state's stringent measures and partly due to the internal discord among the various groups. With too many factions, everyone had a gun, and people started using the movement to fight their petty personal wars. While the movement began as a centralized rebellion spearheaded by JKLF, it soon saw the participation of more radical outfits like Hizb-ul-Mujahideen, Allah Tigers, etc., who began pushing for stricter interpretation of Islam. These outfits openly criticized the Sufi practices prevalent in the valley, such as the tradition of visiting shrines, demanding that Muslim women wear the burkha and Hindu women wear tikas so that their religion was publicly identifiable, and threatened against screening films in theatres. At the same time, security forces intensified their raids to locate hidden militants, leading Kashmir to a point where all civilians were viewed with suspicion. The line between a militant with a gun and a protester with a slogan started disappearing. Both were met with the same bullet. The starkest display of this disappearing line unfolded in 1990.

It all arguably began on 19 January 1990. In the heart of Srinagar, security forces executed sweeping raids in search of militants and concealed weaponry. Approximately 300 individuals, seemingly selected at random, were detained. In the subsequent days, the valley witnessed mass protests as people rallied in bold defiance against the state. The tensions culminated on 21 January at Gaw Kadal in Srinagar. A protest procession was underway when CRPF security forces opened fire. Estimates of the death toll ranged from fifty to hundred, with some victims having been shot, and others, in desperate attempts to evade bullets, jumped off the bridge, only to drown. The horrifying incident at Gaw Kadal prefaced a string of further tragedies that were to occur in 1990. Subsequent events included the BSF firing upon 10,000 protestors in Handwara, resulting in twenty-one deaths and over seventy injuries; security forces attacking protestors in Zakoora and

Tengpur Bypass in Srinagar, leading to nearly forty-seven combined casualties; and the assassination of Mirwaiz Moulana Muhammad Farooq, the mirwaiz of the Jamia Masjid in Srinagar and leader of the Awami Action Committee, by gunmen at his residence, followed by the killing of at least sixty-seven during his funeral procession in the Hawal area of Downtown Srinagar. These incidents underscored a year of escalating violence and mounting tensions in the region.

In 1990, Kashmir had a documented record of hundreds of unarmed civilians being fired upon by the security forces. For those who were not killed, there were widespread arrests, and within the next few years, most localities in Downtown had their own local torture centre. Even on days when there were no raids, fear dominated the public sphere. Militants would seek refuge in the house of the locals, and the locals would fear being found out by the armed forces and having their houses blown up. There were severe repercussions for not cooperating with the militants: people were threatened, looted, and even killed. The idea of a secure home was completely shattered and made out of reach for people in all of Kashmir. Locals reported that they couldn't tell if they would wake up to a raid by militants or the armed forces. Someone I spoke to mentioned that once they found a letter in their drawing room asking for funding for the movement. More jarring than the letter was the fact that someone could so easily walk into their house. Similarly, another person recalled being woken up from his sleep with army jackboots on his mattress. The notions of privacy and security conventionally associated with the idea of home were profoundly compromised for people across the state, and particularly in Downtown. Amidst the relentless physical and psychological turmoil of the 1990s, the very idea of a private space had become unattainable in Kashmir.

Due to the concentration of militants in the area, Downtown often became a battleground between security forces and the militants. Some people who had shifted to other parts of the city discovered that empty properties in Downtown were being used as hideouts by militants or were converted into bunkers by the army. This association of empty properties with ominous events grew among locals who started selling them off. Things were not so different in other parts of Srinagar either. When I met Sameer Hamdani, and we got talking about his formative memories of the city, he vividly recalled a spine-chilling experience he had involving his uncle's empty house in the outskirts of Srinagar. Studying in eleventh grade, as he left in the early hours of the morning for his tuition, Sameer heard a sound similar to that of a halogen lamp bursting and spotted agitated men outside the house. The following day, he learned that someone had been shot in the outhouse the previous day, and the sound he had heard was a gunshot. It was rumoured that the body had been thrown into the nearby lake. Distraught by the tragedy,

city as memory

his uncle decided to dismantle the property, believing it to be tainted by the unjust death. In Kashmir, there's an old saying that when the sky turns red, an innocent life is taken. That day, Sameer says, he felt the weight of its truth.

Farah Bashir's memoir, *Rumours of Spring*, recounting her adolescence in Downtown Srinagar during the 90s, is a powerful account of how violence and fear had become all pervasive in the city. She painstakingly explores the contrasts in the social and spatial experiences of the city during the tehreek and the way the conflict and its associated traumas were percolating into everything that was familiar to her, and rapidly engulfing in its pungent smoke, everything she had seen of life in the twelve years of her existence. Constructing a profound spatial map of her traumas, she walks through the tumultuous transformation of Srinagar:

> I traced the spots from Father's shop to our house, the stretch I had somehow managed to walk through physically unharmed that day. But for the future, I created a map with words that I intended to always carry with me even when my mind froze in fear.
>
> *Zaene Kadal house = Hear jackboots patrolling at five-thirty.*
> *Boher Kadal shop = Bus stop and the spot*

where some militants were released in exchange of Rubaiya Sayeed. She hugged her father who protected her because he could.

1/ When I go straight: Navyut = The bus doesn't stop there anymore. There is no one to pick from the big Kawoosa House. Their daughters and I always competed on the number of windows our houses had. I miss showing off to them. They were forced to vacate as the Indian army took over their house. They turned it into a big bunker.

2/ If I turn left: Saraf Kadal = Close to Razey Kadal, an alternate stop for the school bus to pick us up from, if the usual stop is inaccessible due to crackdown.

3/ If I turn right: Navid Kadal = I never keep any memories from that area. They'd parade my father in front of Mukhbirs there.

Farah draws on her first-hand experiences to offer glimpses into how the concept of safety became entirely disconnected from the idea of home and how intrusions into personal spaces had become the norm in the city. She recalls overhearing a conversation between her mother and aunt about the Kawoosa house, a residential building belonging to an influential family in their neighbourhood being taken over by troops and transformed into a torture centre. Since that day, the ever-present fear that her own house might be subjected to a similar fate constantly weighed on her mind. She recounts a harrowing incident that occurred at her aunt's house in Nigeen, a seemingly safer part of Srinagar where she had gone to spend the night with her cousins. She watched as her young cousins were jolted awake by panic attacks in the middle of the night, while surveillance boats patrolled and flashed lights into their rooms. Incidents like the ones Farah described come up almost naturally in the stories of all those who lived through the 90s in Kashmir when families slept at night in full preparation for midnight raids and women felt compelled to remain modestly dressed even in their most private settings, given the unpredictability of who might enter their homes at any time.

Analysing the impact of such changes on the city at a macro-level, Sameer observes that Srinagar responded to the unprecedented political changes by becoming more insular and mistrustful. During the 1990s and its subsequent fallout, the city underwent significant transformations: life was downscaled, celebrations like weddings were simplified, and residents generally maintained discreet financial profiles. Leisure activities dwindled, and free movement within the city was notably restricted. Residents largely stayed within their immediate vicinities and a trend of constructing gated communities emerged, aimed at deterring militants, protestors, and armed forces from entering their localities. This protective stance was further reflected in the increasing heights of compound walls throughout the city. The era marked a pronounced shift for Srinagar, as it began to fold inward, prioritizing the safety of individual homes and immediate neighbourhoods above all else.

In my father's case, alongside the sweeping political changes he experienced with the rest of the valley, the 90s brought about departures he wasn't prepared for. The Yezdi, which he so cherished, became a source of anxiety. In those days, it wasn't unusual for owners of any means of transport to receive visits from 'unidentified personnel', who could be militants, Ikhwanis, or members of the armed forces, demanding their vehicles for 'missions'. These unidentified visitors were often armed, making refusal not an option. As stories of such incidents in his vicinity grew, my father often found himself waking up in the middle of the night, anxious to check on his beloved Yezdi. Eventually, overwhelmed by the constant anticipation, he sold off 'the first thing he ever loved' in 1993.

÷

Downtown had established itself as the nucleus of the resistance movement in the 1990s, and the revised phase of the movement in the early 2000s saw its resurgence as the centre of political resistance for Kashmir. From 2008 to 2019, Kashmir experienced sporadic cycles of volatility, characterized by massive public demonstrations, stone-pelting incidents, and confrontations with the armed forces. It started in 2008 with the Amarnath Land Row, which saw massive protests against the allocation of forest land to the Shri Amarnathji Shrine Board. Many interpreted this as a violation of Article 35A, leading to nearly sixty-three fatalities. On a similarly large scale, controversy erupted in 2010 following reported 'staged encounters' in the Machil sector by the Indian Army, reigniting Kashmir's demand for self-determination. The 2011 death of young Tufail Mattoo sparked a series of protests, resulting in over 120 deaths. Then, in 2016, the killing of local militant Burhan Wani caused widespread unrest, marked by ninety-six deaths, a continuous curfew that lasted for fifty-one days, and resulted in thousands of injuries, with over 782 eye injuries from the reported use of pellet guns by authorities. Kashmir witnessed a shift from militancy-oriented resistance to street protests and sangbaazi, or stone pelting, which filmmaker and author, Sanjay Kak has called the beginning of a 'new intifada in Kashmir'. While the militant movement hadn't completely died out, the popular shift was towards street protests, with many young men choosing the stone over the gun.

It was hardly surprising that Downtown would take the lead in these civilian uprisings given it had received the most repressive measures by the state after 1989. Most people in the area had had a first-hand experience of personal tragedies in armed conflict, losing friends, family members, and homes. Those who survived had faced intense physical and psychological torture. So, the processions of young men who were willing to risk it all just to throw a few stones at the vast array of troops surprised everyone except those who possessed some context of the brutal and unjust conditions which had shaped their upbringing.

One such person who I could trust to be well informed on the context of the area was Bhavneet Kaur. Having worked on Downtown for over twelve years as a researcher, I could discuss with her the changes the area has been undergoing. Our conversation led us to deliberate upon what had motivated her to focus on Srinagar, particularly Downtown. Based in Delhi, she had landed in the city as a doe-eyed researcher in 2012, holding tight her master's degree in Women Centred Social Work from the Tata Institute of Social Sciences, Mumbai, to write a book on Kashmiri women. As bits and parts of the socio-political situation in the valley started unravelling before her, she realized she was severely underprepared to deal with the nature of the stories she was coming across in the field and the sheer scale of the turmoil and its impact on people. Shelving her plans, she decided to go back to the university to pursue a degree in sociology so that she would be better trained and sensitized to make sense of what she had seen during her fieldwork. In 2015, three years after she had left, Bhavneet returned to Downtown equipped with sociological training and defined research questions to understand how people in Downtown have been making sense of the traumas of the 90s. But now she found the field hostile to the questions she wanted to ask. A unanimous 'bohot bura hua, magar kya faida (whatever

city as memory

happened was terrible, but what was the point)' echoed for months, while she sat in Khanqah, questioning her positionality and the ethics of the whole exercise. Her persistent presence in the community and the personal connections she had developed with people guided her as she navigated Srinagar's tumultuous atmosphere. The past was relived and invoked in all conversations she had with people, whether she was speaking to them for research purposes or not. It is almost impossible to separate the political from the personal in these narratives, as the politics formed the active backdrop that shaped all actions and stories, creating a constant undercurrent of tension. She would glance out of the window of her rented accommodation when someone would point out to her, 'Is spot pey usko goli mari thi jab woh meat lane nikla tha (he had stepped out to buy meat, this is where he was shot)'. Stories like these, where the traumas of the past intertwine with everyday life, provided her brief glimpses into the intimate realities of those living with these memories and their daily repercussions.

Around the same time, with protests intensifying annually and the number of participants growing steadily, the state's response became increasingly aggressive. The militarization of Downtown was escalated. State methods for crowd control included direct firing, the use of pellet guns, and tear gas canisters. Along with the rise in casualties, this period also saw a significant increase in respiratory, cardiac, and psychological health conditions in the valley. In Downtown, clashes between protestors and armed forces became a common occurrence, with areas around Jamia Masjid often looking like war zones especially after the Friday prayers. Bullets, tear gas canisters, and pellets didn't discriminate, catching anyone and everyone who was outside or even peeking out of their homes. Every day, toxic fumes of tear gas choked localities. Reflecting on the continuous exposure to tear gas and its effects on everyday lives, Bhavneet notes in her work:

> The people of Downtown have now incorporated this exceptional experience of *daem* (dum) in their everyday lives as an affliction that they have to live with, as a phenomenological sign of political conflict. It becomes an affliction not only with regard to the public health scare that it generates or immediate loss of life due to toxic gas inhalation but also at the level of embodied affects associated with these violent memories....

After 2008, the term 'Downtown' began to supplant 'Old City' and 'Shahr-e-Khas' in both local vernacular and media reports. While 'Old City' and 'Shahr-e-Khas' invoked a certain nostalgia for Srinagar's rich historical and cultural heritage, 'Downtown' symbolized the area's political, pro-resistance character and the profound turmoil it experienced. In addition to Downtown's connection with the insurgency movement of the 90s, the

city as memory

intense militarization of the area acted as a significant factor in shaping its image as a 'disturbed area'. This perception has been strongly influencing how the rest of the city and Kashmir views the area. It has continued to affect its prospects in business and real estate, and played a part in shaping social and cultural connotations associated with the area, which in turn determines the relationship Downtown shares with the rest of Srinagar.

Bhavneet recalls an episode in 2015 that highlights this complicated relationship. That year, following an encounter in Hyderpor in which some boys, including a young man from Navyut, were killed, violent protests and confrontations between the protestors and armed personnel rocked Downtown. In her attempt to commute to Navyut from Lal Chowk to document the unfolding events, Bhavneet faced dozens of rejections, but eventually, an auto driver she knew agreed to drop her off as close to Navyut as the situation allowed. Upon entering the Baab Dyamb gate, the area appeared deserted, with vacant streets, closed shops, and roads strewn with heaps of stones and broken glass. After a short drive, they spotted a group of men outside some shops and the auto driver left her there, refusing to proceed any further. She recognized someone in the group and informed them of her intention to reach Malaroat so she could be closer to Navyut. Despite their urging her to return due to the uncertainty of the situation, Bhavneet remained adamant. She faces a walking disability, due to which she could not walk the distance, so a young man offered to drop her on his bike. As they rode through the Boher Kadal Road, everything was shuttered, and the only sounds audible were the bursts of tear gas canisters. They were stopped at a security checkpoint manned by heavily armed policemen who signalled aggressively for them to retreat. The biker stopped in front of them and pleaded with the security personnel to allow them to continue, pointing at Bhavneet's disability. Reluctantly, they permitted Bhavneet to proceed while the biker turned back.

Slowly and cautiously, she began her journey, navigating through the Nallah Mar and Boher Kadal Road, heavily patrolled by security forces. They might have intervened to stop her, but she believes that her gender and disability rendered her less threatening to them, granting her a degree of leeway. As she meandered through the lanes, the stories she'd heard during her fieldwork—of people shot while performing everyday tasks—resurfaced in her mind, and she braced for potential danger. Upon nearing the entrance of the Malaroat Road, a group of stray dogs confronted her. Trapped between the dogs and the increasingly impatient security forces, a wave of anxiety overwhelmed her. The subsequent moments became a blur, but she eventually found herself nearing her friend's house. As she neared it, a familiar neighbour rebuked her, shouting out, 'Tum Hindustani yahan humari maut ka tamasha dekhne aate ho, wapis jao. Kyun aayi ho yahan? (You Indians come here to watch our deaths as a spectacle, go back. Why are you here?).'

She managed to reach the home of an older man, an uncle whom she often encountered during her fieldwork. He had been outside and had witnessed his neighbour's outburst. He took her in, and in the subsequent hours, she worked on assessing the situation on the ground. However, as the day progressed and the situation in the streets deteriorated further, the man and his wife suggested that she leave Downtown till the situation improved. Despite his visual impairment, he insisted on escorting Bhavneet to ensure her safety. Accompanied by his wife, they navigated the tense streets, the distinct sounds of windows being latched and hushed conversations about the looming security forces filled the air.

Eventually, when she secured transport out of Downtown and arrived at Lal Chowk, it felt as if she had awakened from a distant dream. There, life continued as usual: roads bustled with traffic, markets were alive with activity, and cafes were brimming with people. The stark disparities between the two sides of the city were evident, as was the unequal distribution of the burden of conflict within the city of turmoil.

÷

A direct outcome of Downtown being viewed as a 'disturbed area' was the growing difficulty for residents to continue living there. Historically, the area was one of the first sites chosen as the capital of Kashmir, witnessing a steady pace of population growth and migration over the past few centuries. However, poor urban planning has left the region highly congested. During the 1950s and early 60s, Bakshi Ghulam Mohammad, the second prime minister of Jammu and Kashmir, initiated a spree of state-building efforts through large-scale infrastructural development and modernization projects in Srinagar. The Civil Lines area on the city's outskirts, intended for the elite to live at a convenient distance from the congestion of the Old City, was also built as a part of these efforts. There was significant internal migration from the Old City to these outskirts during the late 1970s and early 80s, a trend that further intensified over the years. While the primary motivations for this shift were the lack of civic amenities and increasing congestion, the volatile events of the 1990s became a major catalyst. Those with the means began to move away from Downtown, citing safety as their primary concern.

At the height of the militancy movement, Downtown had become the primary battleground between militants and the armed forces. Militants navigated the intricate maze of narrow streets for movement and evasion, often seeking refuge in civilian homes. Subsequently, the local population faced the repercussions of CASO operations and extensive searches. Armed forces would intrude into civilian homes on the slightest suspicion and ransack properties. Moreover, with the rapid emergence of various militant groups, monetary demands from the affluent became commonplace.

Many individuals I interviewed characterized the militancy movement in Kashmir as a struggle between the 'haves and have-nots'. Dr Rashid Maqbool of the University of Kashmir concurred. He emphasized that most global movements of such nature entail a class struggle, and Kashmir was no exception. In the 1990s, the most economically disadvantaged were often the ones enlisted on the frontlines. Concurrently, as the tehreek gained momentum, numerous militant factions solicited financial aid from the well-to-do. The rationale was clear: if the underprivileged were risking their lives, the affluent could at least offer financial support. Consequently, conspicuous consumption became a precursor to trouble. Luxuries like new cars, the latest coloured TVs, or freshly painted houses were signals for different factions to demand contributions.

The escalating demands contributed to a significant outflux of the upper middle class and elites from the area. The ramifications of the 90s insurgency—high incarceration rates, heightened police surveillance, regular confrontations between militants and armed forces, vigilance on the separatist leadership, widespread job losses, and the decline of artisanal industries—led to the sedimentation of classist stereotypes around the area and the people living in it. Downtown became synonymous with urban poverty, deteriorating infrastructure, congestion, illiteracy, and the practice of incarceration of young locals under the Jammu and Kashmir Public Safety Act (PSA), 1978, and other legislative measures. The city's elite deliberately distanced themselves from the area, hoping to avoid entanglement in the ongoing turbulence. Ironically, the people who belonged to the area and had left it looking for better opportunities increasingly started characterizing the area as a 'nuisance' to the normal functioning of the city.

÷

Being one of the primary administrative and commercial centres, the 'disturbed' image of Downtown hurts the interests of the local populations, some of whom have been trying hard to rebrand the place as 'Shahr-e-Khas'. These attempts to revive the Shahr-e-Khas identity of the area aim to use its heritage and history as a counter to the perceptions linked with violence, poverty, and decay. This narrative underscores its deep-rooted connection to Kashmir's historical syncretic traditions, celebrating its stature as a centre for arts and crafts. The state has also been supportive of this through its Smart City initiatives, aiming to counter the widespread perception of Downtown as a pro-resistance stronghold.

This lobbying also intends to stake a claim to the debated concepts of 'Srinagar proper' or the 'real Srinagar', emphasizing its residents as the true shahrik. The debate over who the original inhabitants are remains a fiercely contested and ever-relevant topic in the city. Although Downtown stakes its claim to the title, within its confines, there's no consensus on what exactly constitutes the genuine shahr. The perceptions of shahr have changed drastically with its moving boundaries over generations. Moreover, this equation is complicated by the fact that when the elite mass migrated out of Downtown in the 1980s and 1990s, they took with them the privilege of being called 'shahrik'. This title was used by them to impose a sense of superiority and belongingness over migrants from rural areas and other cities of the valley, who were competing with them for higher economic status and better resources in the city. In my conversations with different sets of people from Srinagar, I noticed a constant qualm that all the original inhabitants of Downtown have left, and only migrants live in the Shahr-e-Khas, thus compromising the cultural purity of the shahr. Popular perceptions like these have played their part in reinforcing classist and casteist stereotypes with Downtown. The convenient (dis)association of the city's elite with Downtown brings to light the class aspect intrinsic to the resistance movement in Kashmir. While the economically vulnerable are glorified as the vanguards of the movement and encouraged to fight the frontline wars, when the overt volatility of the conflict subsides temporarily, the same people are stigmatized and seen as uncultured, illiterate, and drug addicts who pelt stones and hurt the economic and cultural interests of the city.

In my conversation with Mohammad Faysal, who

works as a journalist, he spoke extensively about navigating the stigma of being 'downtownuk'. The fear and shame associated with his Downtown identity, which he vividly remembered feeling as an eight-year-old child standing in a queue to be frisked by soldiers, only intensified with age. When he ventured into the newer, more affluent areas of the city, revealing his Downtown origins became a source of anxiety and embarrassment. Anticipating judgment, he often lied about his roots. As the sense of shame and guilt persisted, he took it upon himself to uncover its source. His journey involved first decoding the basis of this stigma, and then working to redefine the connotations of this label. To achieve the same, he began studying Kashmir's history and tracing the significance of Downtown in popularizing what the region now celebrates—its shawls, papier mâché, literature, Khanqah-e-Maula, woodcarving, and more. Realizing Downtown's centrality in Kashmir's narrative, he took to social media to talk more about the area. Post 2008, his discussions garnered increased attention, especially as Downtown's visibility in the media grew. The fact that much of the separatist leadership, particularly active in the early 2000s, operated from Downtown further accentuated the area's importance in media circles. Taking a step further to address the burden of the classist gaze that he has always felt on himself, he explored the idea of virtual memorization. Faysal now manages a blog titled *Museum of Kashmir*, which he describes as 'an exhibit where people can learn who they are'. The digital museum commemorates memories and other intangible aspects as a way of knowing and remembering Downtown's collective history.

Faysal's memorialization project addresses a very crucial gap that exists between what we know of Downtown through interpersonal conversations and what we see being reflected in official and unofficial documentation. This gap in representation holds true for Kashmir at large. There is no formal memorialization of trauma in Srinagar. Neither the past thirty years of insurgency-related violence, the oppressions under Dogra, Sikh, and Afghan rules, nor the impact of the begari (forced labour) system during the Mughal and Sultanate periods are commemorated. As rulers have changed, victors have planted their flags and run their victory marches through the veins of the city, there are barely any visual and material testimonies of the magnitude of collective trauma that people have gone through. There are no places for people to mourn, process, and make sense of their history. This phenomenon feels more befuddling to the present generations, who have seen different layers of violent realities surface and then disappear without leaving any overt traces in the face of systematic erasures. Srinagar bore the scars of localized torture centres, some of which ceased to function after the late 90s. PAPA 2, a feared torture centre, was transformed into a luxury hotel, while the remnants of another torture centre, Kawoosa House, are gradually being overtaken by commercial establishments. Houses destroyed in encounters were reconstructed, Pandit homes were sold off after years of neglect, and old cinema halls were repurposed as military encampments, almost as if they were destined for such use. Memorials established by the Association of Parents of Disappeared Persons (APDP) for the vanished have been dismantled. In the face of these disappearances, memory and the transmission of oral history become vital for maintaining a connection with the past. Mothers share stories of their missing sons with anyone willing to listen, the houses of torture victims from various centres become landmarks for entire neighbourhoods, such as 'near the house of the man who was tortured at PAPA 2'. Pandit mothers in cramped quarters recount tales of their houses with twenty-two rooms in Srinagar. Witnesses recall the eruption of the joy of the tehreek and also horror that unfolded in the city. People remember the disappearance of once vibrant gardens and orchards from the heart of the city and the burial of the Nalla Mar Canal, once likened to the veins of the city, under layers of concrete. In the absence of written records, collective memory becomes the register. Locations become synonymous with tragedies: Hawal, Gaw Kadal, Chattisingpur. Years are marked by the most tragic events: the year of the Shopian rape case, Machil encounters, the economic blockade, the killing of Burhan Wani, and so on.

Since 2019, there has been a feeling of disquiet over Srinagar like the rest of Kashmir. I find myself unable to read the mood of the city. Is it anger, sadness,

city as memory

dam (suffocation)? During one of my recent visits to Srinagar, I visited Jamia Masjid which had recently been opened for Friday prayers after eighty-nine weeks of closure. Outside, I saw dozens of uniformed men with their guns pointed at the mosque, as men and women flocked inside for prayers. Inside the women's sections, young girls were whispering and hurriedly rushing to the front row. On the loudspeaker, the old imam, with his shaky but assertive voice, intoned, 'Allah.' The women echoed in unison, 'Allah', just the name.

I looked around at the compound of the masjid and the char marks on its roof. It has faced destruction by fire numerous times, and endured bans, and seals, but still, it stood and functioned in enduring glory. I looked at the people in the mosque and thought how their lives too had been ravaged many times: by earthquakes, fires, floods, epidemics, famines, riots, armed violence, and successive rules of invaders and tyrants. As the weight of desolation and collective victimization had started pressing on me, I heard the women echo 'Allah' again as they got up to pray. As I stood up with them, I was reminded of what Faysal had said while concluding our conversation on Srinagar's historical tragedies, 'Of course, there is intergenerational trauma, but you also must see the intergenerational resilience.'

CHAPTER 3
(UN)BELONGING IN THE SHAHR

Srinagar's transition from its medieval past to modernity has been marked by challenges stemming from neglect and oppression by foreign rulers, as well as the internal complexities involved in sustaining political mobilization against them. After a period of relative stability during the Sultanate and the Mughal period, Kashmir saw a long line of weak-willed, self-indulgent autocratic rulers during the Afghan, Sikh, and early Dogra rule who showed very little interest in the region's development and issues of public welfare, and as a result of whose actions, the once promising medieval 'Shahr-e-Kashmir' descended into decay and despondency. The complete disregard for administrative and civic systems left the city grappling with many challenges including neglected drainage and sanitation systems, inadequate supply of clean water, and haphazard town planning. Consequently, the city faced dire outcomes, such as widespread fatalities from the outbreak of epidemics, frequent famines caused by untimely weather conditions, the absence of proper crop storage facilities, and occasional fires that ravaged significant portions of Srinagar. This was made worse by the ruthless taxation policies of the rulers, who levied heavy taxes on the subjects even in the face of abject poverty in the state.

In the latter part of the twentieth century, as the conditions of the administrative affairs and public health had stabilized to a certain extent, and some parts of Srinagar started slowly embarking on their path to urbanization, a host of new challenges awaited the city. Mass uprisings against oppressive state policies which had started in the early decades of the 1900s against the Dogra rulers intensified into a more widespread movement by the end of the century. Kashmir's accession to India in 1947 led to the intensification of pro-freedom mass mobilization, the rise of the armed insurgency movement in 1989, and the repression drive by the state resulted in Kashmir becoming the most militarized region on earth. As a result, the region experienced severe consequences, particularly with the implementation of laws like the AFSPA and PSA, leading to numerous reports of human rights abuses and the curtailment of civil liberties. This tumultuous era also witnessed the tragic mass exodus of the Kashmiri Pandits, the valley's most prominent minority. The volatile political history and unsteady governing regimes in Kashmir have impeded Srinagar's path to urbanization, exacerbating the complexities involved in its shift from a medieval city to a modern urban centre.

Even as these broad events formed the overarching reality that shaped the contextual settings for over 7 million Kashmiris, it's crucial to recognize that the mosaics of their internal, private worlds are more complicated. Their lifeworlds are mediated by various perceptions, memories, and experiences linked with their personal histories and that of Kashmir. In the past centuries, successive generations of Kashmiris have been coming to terms with their rapidly changing political reality to make sense of their precarious circumstances and uncertain futures. However, it is important to remember that the political conflict that has dominated the narratives on Kashmir over the past few decades does not wash over the various forms of social stratification and cultural biases that exist in Srinagar. Like in any other city in the world, life in Srinagar is marred by various forms of stigmatization on the basis of caste, class, gender, sexuality, disability, etc. The presence of conflict doesn't diminish the range of complexities that people encounter in urban areas, whether it's securing dignified accommodation, finding sustainable livelihoods, or cultivating a sense of belonging within the city. Instead, individuals must navigate these intricacies amidst the backdrop of conflict.

In the earlier sections of this chapter, I briefly trace the trajectory of Srinagar's journey to urbanization, and in the later sections, I provide brief glimpses into the complicated lifeworlds of a set of people in Srinagar. While much has been written about the events that have shaped Kashmir's political settings and more detailed personalized accounts exist where people have talked about their experiences, my approach which juxtaposes the lifeworlds of different people from the city seeks to emphasize how the diversity of perceptions, experiences, and memories—which sometimes complement and sometimes contradict each other—have always existed in the city. As individuals share their narratives, recounting personal memories and experiences within the city, these recollections intersect, revealing how individual stories intertwine to weave the intricate fabric of Srinagar.

÷

In his iconic text *History of Srinagar, 1846–1947: A Study in Socio-Cultural Change,* Kashmiri historian Mohammad Ishaq Khan analyses the accounts of Srinagar from various travelogues written in the past couple of centuries to trace how the city has been used to historically narrate the story of Kashmir. Most accounts from the Mughal rule paint a picture of the valley as a developing recreational centre for the Mughal court, and the majority of these records laced with romanticism came from Emperor Jahangir (r. 1605–27), who harboured strong love and admiration for Kashmir's landscape. Jahangir spent fourteen summers of his life in Kashmir, and with him, the entire Mughal court would move to Kashmir, giving Srinagar immense strategic, administrative, and cultural importance. The constant presence of the emperor and his court turned the city into a meeting point for various cultural activities. Poets would arrive from different parts of the Mughal court in Central Asia and Persia to partake in these activities. The percolation of these cultural exchanges into the Kashmiri public sphere was very limited and these exchanges remained restricted to the sections of nobility. Akbar is said to have constructed a great bastioned wall, kalai, around the Haer Parbat and built the complex of his city, Nagar Nagar, inside it. However, the city's construction did not affect the settlement pattern of the rest of Srinagar as its premises remained out of bounds for the local population. In popular memory, the period is most remembered for the set of Mughal gardens—Nishat, Shalimar, Chashme-shahi, and Harwan—considered as remnants from 800 such gardens that existed in Kashmir during the time. The Mughal rule is credited with the establishment of structured bureaucracy in Kashmir, streamlining revenue systems and undertaking maintenance and repairs of bridges built during the Sultanate period, including Habba Kadal, Fateh Kadal, Zaene Kadal, Aael Kadal, and commissioning construction of others, including Safa Kadal. However, outside of their interest in developing Kashmir for their recreational pursuits, they are not remembered for any significant contributions to urban planning and the development of public infrastructure in Kashmir.

During the Afghan rule from 1753–1819, there was some work done for Kashmir's beautification. Some noteworthy projects carried out by governors of the time include the rebuilding of Sona Lank in Dal Lake, reconstruction of the Amira Kadal, and building of the fort of Sherghari and the fort atop Haer Parbat.

city as memory

However, by the time of the late Mughals and Afghans, the elements of romanticism for Kashmir had started diminishing and increasingly the city was being referred to as a congested, unplanned, and filthy space. By the time the Sikhs were ruling Kashmir, the conditions had further degraded with traveller Moorcroft describing the condition of the city in the following terms:

> The general condition of the city of Srinagar is that of a confused mass of ill-favoured buildings, forming a complicated labyrinth of narrow and dirty lanes, scarcely broad enough for a single cart to pass, badly paved, and having a small gutter in the centre full of filth, banked up on each side by a border of mire.

From 1846–90, Srinagar was under Dogra rule, and early rulers like Gulab Singh and Ranbir Singh actively neglected the socio-economic development of Kashmir. Consequently, even the basic minimum facilities, like town planning, drainage systems, sanitation facilities, and water supply management were practically non-existent in the city. In the absence of these, the streets were full of human filth. The contamination seeped into the soil and water bodies, thus making the place prone to cholera and other infectious diseases. Due to frequent cholera outbreaks, Srinagar came to be referred to as 'the centre and nursery of cholera in Kashmir' and 'the city of dreadful death'. The water body networks were also severely affected, with the Jhelum becoming the source of spreading filth and drainage across the city, leading to the choking and silting up of many canals. Things were worse for the poorer quarters of the city including Chattbal and Maisum, which were seen as the 'foyers of the disease' in the city. Within a span of a hundred years, Kashmir saw ten devasting cholera epidemic outbreaks i.e. in 1824, 1844, 1852, 1858, 1867, 1872, 1875–76, 1879, 1888, and in 1892, with the last one killing 5,781 persons in Srinagar, and 5,931 in the other parts of Kashmir. The city's expansion in the absence of state regulations resulted in irregular narrow streets, ill-ventilated and ill-planned houses, congested quarters, defective drainage, and haphazard town planning. Referring to the state of disorder in house planning, British missionary and educator, Cecil Earle Tyndale-Biscoe wrote in 1880: 'Many of the houses were off the straight [sic], often leading one against the other, like two drunken friends supporting each other.'

The general setting of the city was made more unsanitary by the presence of overcrowded burial grounds, unclean slaughterhouses, want of proper surface drainage, dirty cowhouses, slimy tanks, etc. The city overall presented a very grim picture in the face of this neglect.

Urban improvement started in the city around 1886, when the first Municipality Act was passed during Maharaja Pratap Singh's rule. In its earlier years, municipal action was met with severe opposition from the local population of the city, who had gotten used to the squalor and way of life. But with the inclusion of civil society members in the municipality along with the general spread of education and civic sense, people became more accepting of the changes. The municipality undertook the repair of roads and bunds, improvement of drains in different parts of the city, and large-scale public awareness measures. With the improvement in drainage systems, successful sanitation drives, and improved water work systems, even as cholera hit the city multiple times between 1900 and 1929, its impact was more contained than the earlier episodes. Additionally, with the establishment of the British Residency in Srinagar in 1885, road connectivity had received a major boost with the construction of the Jhelum Valley Cart Road from Kohala to Baramulla in 1889. It was extended to Srinagar in 1897. Running roughly around 315 kilometres, the road was a major step towards building a sustainable communication network in the valley and ending Kashmir's geographical isolation. With the road, the distance between Srinagar and Rawalpindi could be covered in one day by motor and in around four days in a tonga. This was a major improvement for connectivity, given previously when dongas had been the only mode of transport, it would take people twenty-four hours just to travel from Srinagar to Baramulla through water transport.

As the situation in the city was improving, the suburbs still presented an active threat of infectious diseases in the city. Petitions were made to include them in the jurisdiction of the Srinagar municipality so that effective action could be taken to curb the spread of diseases. Consequently, the suburbs of Buchpur and Zaedbal were added in 1915, and the areas of the Zuenmar track including Batmalyun, Sonwaer, Shivpur, Rathpur, Bagh Nand Singh, and Bonamsar were included in the limits of the city between 1921–23. During this period, Kashmir was also witnessing large-scale migration from rural areas into the city. Rural migration to Srinagar had been a trend for centuries, as exemplified by Walter Lawrence's account regarding the famine of 1877–79, when he had observed that 'people were migrating to escape from forced labour and to obtain cheap food'. However, with the improvements in Srinagar's standard of living, the scale of migration also increased. Along with better civic facilities, Srinagar began offering newer employment opportunities in industries such as wool, silk, hospitality, electric installations, as well as in the neighbouring quarries for road and metal. In 1901, the Srinagar silk factory alone employed nearly 7,000 persons.

Commenting on the cultural implication of this change, Ishaq Khan states, 'The city not only provided employment to the labourers from the villages but also it changed the way of life of the rural people living in its hinterland. With the growth of the tourism industry, Srinagar's increased demand for food-stuffs and a workforce tied the surrounding areas even more closely to the economy of the city.' Nearby villages began to focus on dairy, poultry keeping, and market gardening to meet the urban demand for milk, fruits, and vegetables. The villagers tapped into the medical, educational, and recreational facilities available in the city. As a result, more money flowed through the neighbouring villages, leading to their gradual urbanization. These shifts acted as catalysts for socio-cultural changes. As the villages and the shahr converged due to shared economic interests, a clash of sensibilities emerged. A consequence of this was that the shahri identity began establishing a distinction for itself, equating itself with culture and sophistication, while looking down upon the 'gaam' as culturally deficient. Relatedly, the shahri identity started asserting their claims to the city as being its 'asli' inhabitants, to solidify their sense of belonging, and deny it to those who were coming into the fold of the expanding city.

As the improved sanitary conditions along with the boost in connectivity aided Srinagar's path to modernity, the city witnessed a higher influx of outside visitors in the form of English officers, travellers, and missionaries. These exchanges significantly influenced the city's culture and its aspirations. The period saw Srinagar take steps towards incorporating features that were expected of modern cities in the twentieth century, including metalled roads, masonry bridges, solid embankments, and electric lights. It also saw the inauguration of the land settlement and the reorganization of the Financial,

Public Works, Postal Telegraph, and Forest departments which contributed a great deal to the administrative aspects of Srinagar's modernization project. While the Old City continued to remain heavily dependent on small-scale artisanal industries, the affluent class of government employees started moving toward the newly developed Civil Lines area of the city which included areas like Lal Chowk, Polo View, Maulana Azad Road, Regal Chowk, Raj Bagh, Jawahar Nagar, Gogji Bagh, Wazir Bagh, Karan Nagar, etc. The Civil Lines area specifically established itself as the centre of elite urbanity in Srinagar. These areas contained material testimonies to Srinagar's urbanization in the form of footpaths, cinema halls, missionary schools, hospitals, wider roads, bigger markets, better accessibility to public transport, and public parks. By 1920, women in purdah would flock to Pratap Park for recreation and the trend of picnics and garden parties was also established.

Congestion, bad roads, and lack of civic facilities had started driving the well-heeled families out of the Old City. Those who had the capital started moving to newer localities like Jawahar Nagar, Wazir Bagh, Raj Bagh, Sonwar, and Ram Munshi Bagh. The 1980s saw an increase in the outward migration patterns from the Old City, but the insurgency movement and the subsequent militarization of Old City triggered mass migration towards different suburbs of Srinagar. This phenomenon where the original inhabitants left the Old City on a massive scale had complex implications for the notions of being a shahri and the pride associated with the identity. For a lot of people from Downtown, moving out was a traumatic event, and the move to suburban areas was considered a degradation from their shahri status. During my conversation on the subject with researcher and educator, Gowhar Fazili, he spoke of his friend whose family had moved from Downtown to Naseem Bagh in the outskirts of the city in the 1990s. Both his paternal and maternal houses were in Downtown, so when he moved away from Srinagar, his social connections disappeared. With both his parents working, there were no neighbours and relatives he could speak to, and a bleak sense of loneliness encompassed him. Gowhar says his friend found the pastoral setting, with sunbaked cakes of cowdung all around, to be a marker of declassing. The belief that a natural setting inherently represents tranquillity is a culturally constructed perception. While many idealize pristine green landscapes, for others, including his friend, this greenery was invariably associated with the idea of a village that primarily symbolized bleak primitiveness rather than serenity. His friend could never mend the bond with his parents, whom he blamed for the move that severed his formative association with his home in Downtown. Gowhar's friend was not the only one who felt this way. I chanced upon Mujtaba Kadri at the Mahatta Diner Cafe in Lal Chowk while conducting an interview with Sameer Hamdani. Joining the ongoing conversation, Mujtaba discussed his family's relocation from Downtown to the outskirts in Nishat. His initial impressions of the new place likened it to a 'dead village'. He noted significant cultural differences between their values and those of the local villagers. The coexistence felt more like a degradation to him. He hated his new surroundings so much that he would leave his Nishat home in the morning, spend the day in Downtown, and return only at night. It is interesting that even though the distance from the outskirts to the shahr wasn't considerable, many people saw this as diminution of their cultural and social status. This was the case even when such moves were made voluntarily.

By the 2000s, the outskirts of the city witnessed a huge influx of migrants from other parts of Kashmir, who preferred to settle down on the peripheries closer to their home districts to retain spatial proximity and a sense of connection with their ancestral areas. It was during this time that the areas in the outskirts of Srinagar like Hyderpor, HMT, and Peerbagh started becoming populated. As the composition of the city increased in its complexity, many fractured notions of belongingness started emerging. With the majority of the middle- and upper-middle-class populations relocating from Downtown, the poorer segments were left behind, to face the aftermath of the insurgency and the public protests in the 2000s. Downtown was being increasingly perceived as the hub of disturbances. The population that dispersed from Downtown resettled in various parts of the city. To differentiate themselves from the migrants in these new areas, the cultural distinction of being an 'asli shahruk' began to be emphasized more pronouncedly. The absence of this currency came to be used to question their place and sense of belonging to the city. It led me back to what Sameer said of the city, 'The city sees itself as "imtiaz mizaaz (a superior disposition)". It sees itself as the enabler of modernity and a privileged space. The people of the city see themselves as enablers of everything that is Kashmiri culture, which is why you have the gaam–shahr divide. It's ironic that most of these people are not even part of that physical space of the city, as they have moved to the suburbs. So, it is interesting to see what that has done to notions of shahr and being a shahri.'

Differences in sensibilities and ways of relating to the city stem from various historical, economic, and socio-cultural factors and play a vital role in shaping distinct perceptions of the city for the inhabitants. The question of what determines a person's sense of belonging to the city is a perpetually evolving concept, with answers that shift depending on whom you ask. The elites relate to Downtown only to authenticate their claim to their original shahriness but are quick to distance themselves from what the area represents now. The lack of ancestral connection with the shahr is used to question, mock, and delegitimize the experiences and belongingness of those who have migrated to the city. The migrants are accused of being opportunistic, not participating in the residents' struggle, diluting the shahri identity with their 'gaam' cultures, and building their localities on wetlands, thereby choking the city and degrading its ecology. However, for the migrants, some of whom have lived in the city for decades, it is a frustrating ordeal that they still don't find themselves being accepted by the city, even as they significantly contribute to the city's economy, culture, and appeal. While the trajectory of how these stereotypes came to be can be traced, that is not my primary point of interest. I shift my lens to look at how these stereotypes inform the lifeworlds of different people in the city and shape their sense of belonging in Srinagar.

÷

While the uptown and Downtown areas are often portrayed as two primary urban blocks with distinct subcultures, this simplistic binary overlooks the historical complexity of numerous neighbourhoods like Hawal, Zaedbal, Lal Bazar, and others. Take the case of Zaedbal. The area is one of the largest settlements of Shia Muslims in Kashmir and holds immense religious, cultural, and historical importance to the community. The first imambada was established in the area in 1518. Shamsuddin Araqi, a medieval Sufi saint remembered for popularizing Shia Islam in Kashmir, also set the centre for his tabligh (preaching) in Zaedbal. Despite this, since the area is geographically located on the periphery of the Old City, its claim to being part of the actual shahr has been contested historically and culturally.

Based in the area, Dr Rashid Maqbool tells me how the term 'sarhaedi' was used by people from the shahr to mockingly refer to those who used to live in peripheral areas. Derived from the term 'sarhad' meaning border, the term and its connotation significantly contributed to his perception of the city and his place in it. Although used teasingly, the term served to enforce a distinction on the basis of class, culture, and urbaneness, and segregated those who lacked these shahri sensibilities as a separate group of people. He added that if someone looks at Srinagar from the outside, they would think of the whole city as the shahr, but internally there are many imaginary boundaries at play. Some of these biases draw upon administrative and geographical boundaries that existed historically in the city. Many of these areas used to fall outside the municipal jurisdiction of Srinagar and were only incorporated into the fold of the district at a later stage. However, cultural perceptions around the area have not evolved to reflect these changes.

Even though these areas were merged administratively with the city, they still did not fit into the tassavur (imagination) of the shahr for many people. This tassavur has been seen as the cultural monopoly of the Shahr-e-Khas. People who lived in parts of the Old City like Amira Kadal, Habba Kadal, or Fateh Kadal had easier access to the currency of urbanization owing to their proximity to Civil Lines, Lal Chowk, and the upcoming uptown in the city. As a result, people in these localities developed some urban sensibilities which the peripheral areas were distanced from. The difference was further consolidated by their access to markers of affluence like the presence of missionary schools, hospitals, shops, and better public transportation. Concomitantly, detachment from these markers intensified the feeling of being sarhaedi in areas like Zaedbal. However, Dr Rashid points out that the term had fallen into disuse by the mid-1990s, for a variety of reasons.

With improvements in transport and the expansion of markets into inner links of the area, the line of the sarhad had started blurring. This was accompanied by the rise of English-medium schools throughout the city, which sought to address the gap between elite missionary schools and Urdu-medium government schools. With the larger democratization of the English language in the city, a new middle class was consolidating by the late 80s. With improved access to the vocabulary and props of modernization, they were in a better position to counter the stereotypes associated with their so-called sarhaedi sensibilities. The insurgency movement and its suppression also had a profound influence on these cultural notions. The city became very inward-looking, with everyone focussing on their safety and bare survival. During this time, the changes that were taking place at the macro level in the city were not being realized because everyone was confined to their house. The city did not have the basic minimum conditions of normalcy that would have allowed the people to experience the shifting notions of urbanism and modernity. So, for a period of ten to fifteen years, as the city struggled for sustenance, different notions of urbanity were dying and re-emerging without people actively realizing. The idea of being a sarhaedi within the city was one of them.

This notion of the sarhaedi, however, was not applicable to all Shias. A small population of prominent and educated Shia families lived in the Old City in the 1920s, particularly in areas like Namchibal, Habba Kadal, and Fateh Kadal. Kashmiri-American poet, Agha Shahid Ali's family was one of them. Economically well-off Shia families like these had access to cultural influences from both Pandits and elite Sunni Muslims, so their way of life and the nature of engagement with Kashmir was different from the Shias of Zaedbal. So, while the cultural perceptions around Zaedbal came to be associated with orthodoxy and radical, primitive thinking, the Shias of uptown who were more readily assimilating with other populations came to be associated with progressive thinking. Dr Rashid added more nuance to the conversation by pointing out that despite the sectarian differences that were at play between the Shia and Sunni communities which would lead to clashes, especially during Muharram, differences between the communities are not homogenous in nature. Within communities, individuals often coalesced based on shared economic interests and similar sensibilities. For instance, elite Shias from uptown found greater affinity with their Sunni counterparts than with Shia groups from suburban areas. In the same vein, among artisans in the papier mâché, shawl, and carpet weaving sectors, common economic pursuits brought Shias and Sunnis of the same economic tier closer together, often more so than with individuals of differing economic statuses within their respective sects. However, this is not to say that the Shias in the valley are not unified in their history of marginalization and persecution. According to Dr Rashid, in Kashmiri Shia sensibilities, the sense of persecution is derived from two main frames: one is the global, pan-Islamic frame, rooted in the tragic events involving Hussain and his family in Karbala. The second draws from Kashmir's local history, particularly the suppression of the Chaks by the Mughals and the subsequent atrocities inflicted upon the sect by Afghan rulers. Together, they play out in a myriad of ways for the community.

Within his personal experiences, he holds vivid memories of feeling deeply marginalized as a Shia while traversing the city. Even though he lacked the vocabulary to fully understand it, the unease he felt when visiting Sunni mosques, his hesitation to use his turbah (the stone Shias use for prayers) in public spaces, and the common stereotypes about his community all collectively shaped his anxieties and perceptions about his identity. Such experiences are echoed by many in the community, which is why Shias tend to congregate in specific clusters across Kashmir, be it in distinct villages or colonies within particular urban localities.

These anxieties are historically justified. In his work *Shi'ism in Kashmir: A History of Sunni–Shi'i Rivalry and Reconciliation*, Sameer notes a gradual retreat of Shias from the city's public affairs due to a series of communal clashes that disproportionately affected their localities and places of worship over the past centuries. After the 1830 riots, many Shias fled from areas such as Malkah-Shampur, Hasanabad, and Zaedbal and took refuge within the secluded confines of the Dal Lake. This self-imposed seclusion gave birth to a unique lifestyle deeply intertwined with the lake. This shift also resulted in the community losing access to several communal skills. Even with this migration, some Shia pockets persisted and managed to thrive amidst challenges. While occupation-based spatial arrangements have historically existed in Kashmir, a significant consequence of Shias living in close-knit communities is the retention of certain crafts, like papier mâché, as being predominantly associated with the Shias. Consequently, the mohallas of Hasanabad, Kamangarpur, and Zaedbal have evolved into centres of excellence for papier mâché craftsmanship.

Known for his mastery in papier mâché, Fayaz Ahmad Jaan is one such artist whose craft was shaped in the vocational hub of Hasanabad. As a craftsman deeply connected to the trade, he attributes the craft's lineage to the Shia belief system, crediting Mir Sayyid Ali Hamadani (also known as Shah-i-Hamadan). While historical sources predominantly attribute the introduction of the craft to Kashmir to Sultan Zain-ul-Abidin, who brought in experts from Samarkand in the fifteenth century, local narratives associate its popularization with Mir Sayyid Ali Hamadani. According to these accounts, Hamadani is believed to have arrived in Kashmir with 700 craftsmen from Persia, imparting the art of papier mâché to the local Kashmiris. Introduced to the art by his father at the mere age of four, Jaan recounts stories that he had heard from his father, where the fervour for originality was so intense that craftsmen would shield their designs from prying eyes by pulling the curtains shut on their workshop every time a visitor came. This was done to prevent any accidental glimpses and avoiding potential imitations.

The community's inclination to cluster together was also evident during the outward migration from Downtown in the late 80s and 90s. Most Shia families gravitated towards areas like Lal Bazar and Bhagwanpor, which already had significant Shia influence. Even in the city's outskirts, members of the community prefer to reside in closely-knit neighbourhoods, often identified by insignia used by members of the Shia community globally such as black flags and photos of religious leaders from Iran.

÷

Given the shahri identity has been on guard against those who are settling down in the city, it comes as no surprise that the migrants feel a sense of alienation and disconnectedness in Srinagar even after spending decades of their life there. Mariyeh Mushtaq, a researcher and visual artist, has lived in Srinagar all her life. Her parents migrated there from Kupwor more than thirty-five years ago, but for her, Kupwor is still 'ghar' and Srinagar is 'shahr'. This difference in the association is not caused by her relationship with Kupwor as much as it had to do with a feeling of 'unbelongingness' that has been central to her relationship with the city. Even before she had the language to understand the city, she felt the implications of the shahr–gaam divide influencing her interactions with the city. The fact that she lived in Peerbagh, one of the more affluent parts of the city, and went to private school didn't help mitigate this. She says that people in Srinagar have this habit of asking you, 'Aap asli kahan ke ho? Nahi *originally* kahan sey ho (Where are you really from? No, where are you from *originally*)?' People keep analysing you, looking for the tinge of accent in your tone. They look for cues and mentions of other places in the conversation in an attempt to place you. For them, any and all associations with places outside the shahr are a subject of disdain. People who have lived in the city for decades express a fear of being 'found out' and having their connections to their native places exposed, which are then used to undermine their claims of being true 'shahri'. Mariyeh adds, 'For people from Kupwor, the idea they have is that they are "gaamik greese"'.

She picked up on it in her early childhood, so whenever someone *originally* from Srinagar would ask her where she was *actually* from, she would say Sopore instead of Kupwor thinking that since Sopore is a town they might somehow think is better. However, it took her time to realize that for people from Srinagar, everything outside Srinagar is one blob of ruralness. Their cultural perception places shahr as the nucleus of urbanity, which is surrounded by an undifferentiated mass of territories that get subsumed under the monolithic category of the gaam.

Mariyeh recalls a childhood incident that encapsulates how this feeling of unbelonging is planted into the consciousness of those whose place in the city is not justified by their family lineage but through migration for better opportunities and facilities. In a noisy classroom, Mariyeh had retorted to a teacher who had singled her out for creating noise. Angered by her brazenness, she asked her:

'Kahan sey ho (Where are you from)?'

'Peerbagh.'

'Nahi asli kahan sey ho (No, where are you from *originally*)?'

'Sopore.'

'Hmm, lagta hai, lagta hai (Hmm, looks like it, looks like it).'

Mariyeh became suddenly very conscious about what part of her brought out the 'gaam' in her personality. Her friends surrounded her and said consolingly, 'Yeh

city as memory

pagal hai, tu nahi lagti hai gamech (She is crazy; you don't look like you are from a village).' Currently based in Istanbul, Mariyeh is the editor of *ZanaanWanan*, an independent feminist collective and action research group based in Srinagar and the visual artist behind Kashmir Pop Art, an award-winning mixed-method art project. She looks back at the well-meaning consolation attempts by her friends with a laugh. It is clear to her now that the teacher had already decided to place her outside of what she thought was the civilized shahr. Mariyeh could have answered Anantnag, Varmul, Pulwama, Handwara, Kupwor, or any other part of the valley, but her scornful, 'Hmm, lagta hai, lagta hai' would have remained the same.

Mariyeh's experiences are also reflected in different generations of migrant experiences in the city. Dr Ayesha is from Varmul and works as a gynaecologist in the biggest and busiest maternity hospital in Kashmir. As a young and accomplished doctor who visually presents signs of affluence that one can associate with urbanity, she says this 'gaam' scorn is thrown at her mostly by men whenever they feel intimidated or threatened by her. 'Angry attendants do it all the time,' she says lightheartedly. Once when she had left her car parked outside a shop in Srinagar, the shopkeeper looked at her number plate which read JK05 (indicating a vehicle registered in Varmul) and he started screaming at her, 'Tum gaon ke log pata na kahan sey paisa kama kar yeh gadiya latay ho aur humare sar pe chadatay ho (Don't know where you villagers get the money to buy these cars from, and then you make them our problem).' The gaam connection springs up in the most surprising ways.

If Srinagar looks down on the gaam(s) as the site of primitiveness, the gaam looks at the city as a space of haughtiness, shrewdness, and cunningness. Shagufta migrated to Srinagar forty years ago and lives in one of the affluent parts of the city. Yet while looking for a match for her son, her specific instructions to the maenzemyor (matchmaker) were to find them a girl who is based in Srinagar, but is originally from the gaam. The reason being that a 'shahri ladki' would always have lauded her shahriness over her son. Similarly, when Mariyeh decided to marry someone *originally* from Srinagar, her family had to go around convincing her extended family and friends in Kupwor that although they are shahrik, they are also nice people.

Another point of contention that undermines the claim to shahriness of those from uptown colonies is their perceived limited involvement in the resistance movement. Mariyeh agrees that there is a clear disparity when it comes to public participation in such movements, and there are different socio-cultural reasons for the same. In places like Peerbagh which have been recently populated, people from different parts of Kashmir have settled over the past few decades, and there is no deeper set of community values or shared experiences that tie them together. This is unlike Downtown, where people have an intergenerational connection with their neighbours and community members. In these newly formed settlements people interact with each other on very impersonal lines. These localities have been populated by upper-middle-class migrants like bureaucrats, government employees, doctors, and engineers, and the priority has been on securing their economic bases and position in the city. Mariyeh says that a lot of these migrant families had to face the stress of starting a life in a completely different city, so most of them never got around to prioritizing the community aspect of their lives. Even after thirty years in the city, her mother still tells them that 'aes ayi wapar mulkas manz (it feels like we migrated to an alien country)' for their education. Her mother, who has worked as a government teacher all her life, had to go through a journey to be accepted in her profession. She was aware that shahri teachers were looking down upon her because of her gaam connection. So, she went out of her way to stay updated on current trends to show people she was well-informed, and in this way, she earned their respect. She had to constantly prove herself to the shahri gaze. Since the first generation of migrants faced issues in being accepted to the city, they actively prioritized better education and stable jobs for their children. Consequently, engagement in socio-political matters has been of tertiary focus and often actively discouraged in a lot of middle- and upper-middle-class families, for it can potentially come in the way of getting government jobs.

÷

Gowhar Fazili has lived between Srinagar, Bengaluru, and Delhi all his life. His primary relationship with Srinagar has been that of curiosity and inquisitiveness. This spirit of inquiry, accompanied by concerns about the intellectual trajectory of Kashmir's popular movement for selfhood has kept him tied to the valley, even as vocalization of some of the concerns about ethical and effective strategies for achieving such an end resulted in a near fatal attempt on his life in his own house. His family was one of the first to move out of Downtown to the outskirts of the city in the mid-1970s. Despite being only two years old when they relocated from Navid Kadal, Downtown, to Buchpur, he vividly remembers the contrasting impressions that the two places left on his mind. Out from the congested, dingy, and dark lanes of Downtown, the willows, streams, paddy fields, and apple orchards in Buchpur felt like a dream to him. Theirs was one of the first few houses in the new settlement that was developing in Buchpur where the people shifting out of congested Downtown were beginning to settle. The new neighbourhood that was emerging remained aloof and distinct from the original village that existed in the neighbourhood. People were purchasing and developing properties in a manner that allowed them to remain distinct from the village and retain a veneer of modernity and association with their neighbours and relatives from Downtown and other ancestral locations. However, in the 1990s, as the state started coming down hard, the large-scale and haphazard nature of migration from Downtown broke the class-caste boundaries that the earlier settlers had sought to maintain. As his matamaal continued to be in Downtown, his entire childhood was spent experiencing the contrasts between the two parts of the city.

In his mother's youth, his matamaal was humorously known as the 'railway station' because all the ladies from the outskirts of the city would frequently land up there, drop their kids and burkhas, and go off shopping. While it was always crowded and had no strict notion of privacy or personal space, he remembers it as a place of familial warmth and absolute freedom where he could land up at a neighbour's or relative's house and it wouldn't be thought of as unsafe or intrusive. His life in Buchpur was different in comparison. He and his siblings were not allowed to mix with local children from the area—a rural setting with no markets and no hawkers, no sounds of small industries of coppersmiths, bakers, and potters to fill the soundscape, and only the chirping of birds, gurgling of streams, and the rustling of trees and paddy in the wind. Even though in Downtown they would at times share a room with ten cousins, in this new place, he and his siblings found themselves scattered in their separate rooms at the earliest opportunity. In the 1990s, tehreek became a trigger for his remaining relatives in Downtown to move out and relocate to Buchpur. Although the people he was associated with shifted closer to his home, he feels that the warmth and sense of community was not recreated in the new houses. 'It is the culture associated with the place that you perhaps cannot recreate,' he says wistfully.

As was the case with several middle- and upper-middle-class parents situated away from Downtown, Gowhar's parents made active attempts to shield him from what was happening in the city, and this meant keeping him uninformed about the political history of the place and the events that were unfolding in Kashmir. Any attempt to satisfy his curiosity about the issue was met with angry dismissal and threats of punishment. However, as the unrest spread, he defiantly ventured out to meet older people in the neighbourhood who held strong opinions on what was unfolding in the valley. He vividly remembers the first time he saw a tiny JKLF sticker affixed to the railing of the SP College gate where he had gone for his practical exams. He was really surprised at the sight of it, so he took it off and kept it in his book. While Gowhar wanted to understand the social and political dynamics of the city, his father wanted him to stay away from what he saw as invitation to trouble and pushed him to pursue a professional career in medicine or engineering. This resulted in frequent fights between the two. Because of the tense situation, it was decided that it would be best for him to go away from home. This was happening in the broader context of 'catch-and-kill' policy where young boys were being arrested and killed and being passed off as militants, and as a teenager, he was vulnerable. Moreover, his quest for inquiry was not helping his chances. So, he moved to Bengaluru and Delhi for studies hoping for things to get better at home and in his hometown in the meanwhile. While Gowhar visited home during the short summer breaks, the period he spent away from Kashmir lasted nine long years.

Even though he had physically moved away from the place, the questions about what had happened to his place, why it had happened, and what must be done to shape a better future continued to haunt him. Gowhar took up social sciences, to understand the world and to see how societies have previously dealt with similar situations. During his time in Bengaluru and Delhi, his exposure to academics and the liberal intellectual culture of the cities made him more confident and gave him a new vocabulary and ways of thinking about society. He came back to Kashmir, helped revive an environmental organization called Green Kashmir, and started teaching Political Science at Women's College. He simultaneously ran an initiative called SPACE, which was an open platform for experiential learning. Through this platform, he and his students discussed philosophical and political questions pertaining to the history and future of Kashmir, apart from the personal struggles that come with living in a troubled world. The platform engaged in conversations on the objectives of the ongoing struggle, posing fundamental questions like how the future society they envisaged would deal differently with the minorities and others who do not belong to the dominant gender, culture, and religion. It recognized the need to acknowledge the use of religious symbolism in the movement for azaadi and assess its impact on minorities. It reviewed questions like the Pandit exodus and tried to host meetings between Pandits and Muslims in Jammu and Srinagar. During such conversations, Gowhar remembers how charged-up young people would exclaim, 'Hum sirf baatien hi kartien hain, kuch kartay nahi hain (We only talk, we don't do anything)', and he would calm them down by saying, 'Baatien karo, baat karna aur sochna sab se badi action hai (Talk; talking and thinking is the most important action).' 'We readily embrace action, but thinking is the hardest thing,' he emphasized. He, along with his colleagues, ran SPACE till 2004, for close to three years, before unidentified persons broke into his house and lodged four bullets into his body.

He still doesn't know who shot him, but he believes it could have been people from either side. He admits that after being largely away for nine years, he was out of sync with the situation in Kashmir. While he had acquired the language to initiate a number of critical conversations, retrospectively, he feels he was reckless in his attempts to start such conversations in Kashmir without ascertaining if the time was right. Though there had been a considerable drop in violence during those years, many unidentified state and non-state actors were at play in the valley, and it is likely Gowhar managed to upset one group or the other. He also feels that because he spent most of the 90s outside Kashmir, when he returned to Kashmir in 1999 and attempted his social interventions, people started to question his motivation.

'But then I have always struggled to make friends with people,' he says, taking a light-hearted diversion from this visibly traumatic incident, sipping his coffee while busily texting his students. 'I did not have many friends in school, so I had to make do with other social rejects like me. Such social awkwardness and exclusion shapes your politics from an early age, it makes you see things from the point of view of the marginalized. When I was in school, I co-started a club with other social rejects—the Pentagon Sports Club—which had only five people: two Pandits, two Sunnis, and a Shia. No one would play with us, so we played with each other, away from the popular kids who preferred cricket and sometimes met even after the school hours. If any other person was rejected from the main playgroups, they would join us. The year 1989 was supposed to be a big one for the Pentagon Club, when we were collectively supposed to purchase our first synthetic football. We had collected ₹192 and needed to achieve the target of ₹210 or something to be able to buy one. But suddenly, the tehreek happened. Soon the Pandits, including our treasurer left, and along with many other things, that was the end of the Pentagon Sports Club,' he smiled. The more I spoke to people, the more I was certain that the casualties of conflict cannot be quantified.

Like Gowhar's accounts, most recollections of the Pandit exodus from non-Pandits describe the mass departure as an event that occurred with an unexpected abruptness, shocking everyone. However, most Kashmiri Pandits are now retrospectively able to recollect the subtle yet ominous signs that had begun to unfold by the end of the 1980s. I was in twelfth grade when I visited a Pandit house for the first time. It was in a migrant camp in Jammu, and my friend's father's colleague, Sandeep Uncle, had invited us for lunch. As uncle drove us in his car, the music system played Kashmiri songs that I had never heard. In his house, his sari-clad mother and wife greeted us warmly. We spoke in Urdu; they responded in Kashmiri. As my friend Asma and I looked around the house, we were fascinated to see Kashmiri and Hindu symbols placed in harmony together. Each time Sandeep Uncle's mother spoke in Kashmiri, my gaze would shift to the bindi on her forehead, her sari, and the dejhoor chain running through her ear. While I had seen these markers of difference in photographs and on TV, they had been relegated in my mind as insignia of the other. I was grossly underprepared for the range of feelings: intimacy, tenderness, separation, pain, and loss I felt towards the other who spoke my language. *She is like me.*

Decades later, I found myself sitting across from Vivek Raina in his office in New Delhi, bracing for what I anticipated would be a weighty conversation.

city as memory

Instead, I was surprised by his spirited demeanour and the manner in which he guided our discussion through various aspects of our shared identity and history. We found ourselves discussing Kashmir's socialist past and his grandfather's passion for the movement. He even shared a socialist interpretation of the well-known Kashmiri folksong, 'Bumburo Bumburo'. 'You think it's just about the lover and the beloved, but in Kashmiri language, nothing has just one interpretation,' he said excitedly.

Our conversations seamlessly moved between three languages and even though we had never met before and were separated by a generational gap, certain words from Kashmir invoked within us a familiar mix of awe and dread. *He is like me.* This act of situating myself in the other for relatability is a narcissistic act, but for people of a divided and segmented homeland like ours, it is the beginning of understanding the other. Rahul Pandita makes a reference to how truths became different for the two communities post 1989–90. While addressing the contradictions of those truths, Vivek and I tried to peek into the common past that lay behind the haze of the early 1990s.

But even as we attempted to delve into our common past, the events of the early 1990s could not be sidestepped or glossed over by the ideals of Kashmiriyat or narratives of cultural syncretism and communal harmony. As we got talking, retrospectively, Vivek could identify the changes in his everyday life that had hinted at ominous developments in the future. The earliest memories he recalls are fragmented in his mind: the cancellation of the school's annual day programme after months of practice, the arrest of separatist leader Shabir Shah and the widespread reaction it elicited, and the bomb blast at the General Post Office in Lal Chowk, where his aunt's neighbour was injured.

After this, around 1988–99, he had started hearing about the targeted killings of Pandits such as that of Justice Neel Kanth Ganju and other prominent figures. However, neither he nor his family felt threatened because all of the targets had been influential people, and they continued in the hope that this would not affect them. He vividly recalls the time he heard the demand for azaadi for the first time on the streets of Srinagar. Some boys from his school were pelting stones nearby, and some people came out of their houses and started thrashing them. The elders asked them why they were pelting stones, and they said, 'for azaadi'. Some of his classmates also started telling him about how there is a fight in the Maisum side of the city every day, where people throw stones and everybody runs, suggesting they go as well. Gradually, rumours about the cross-border movement from Pakistan and guns being supplied to locals started circulating, but even then, Vivek's sense of normalcy was intact.

The situation escalated when Rubaiya Sayeed was kidnapped, sparking some amount of condemnation internally within the communities. However, when the

JKLF militants were released, Vivek witnessed mass euphoria on the streets. He feels that while there had been some ambitions and emotions regarding azaadi earlier, the crumbling of the state infused hope in people; not just in some sections, but there was mass hope. Merely three days later, he remembers how the chanting in the mosques started, and there was a clear articulation of the demands for azaadi. Along with the chants for azaadi, they also started hearing slogans like, 'Azaadi ka matlab kya, la ilaha illallah (What does Azaadi mean? There is no god but Allah)' and 'Yahan kya chalega? Nizam-e-Mustafa la sharqiya la garbiya, Islamia (What will work here? The rule of Mustafa. No eastern, no western, only Islamic rule, only Islamic rule)'. This is when the alarm bells for his family started going off. As the sloganeering and processions continued through the night, they couldn't sleep. Around midnight, they started hearing the sounds of the armed police firing on crowds. And within no time, this escalated and became a regular event in the city. Even then, his family had not considered leaving Kashmir.

By this time, many Pandit families had left. Vivek remembers how his aunt from Habba Kadal was leaving for Jammu too, and she offered to take Vivek with her. His father had scoffed at the suggestion, stating that Vivek had tuition classes in Kashmir and couldn't afford to waste time. However, things escalated rapidly, and within fifteen days from this incident, they too left for Jammu. What had kept Vivek and his family afloat was the belief that while there had been killings, they had been for Pandits and Muslims, and most of them had been influential people with some connection to positions of power. However, the social circles of victims soon began to overlap with theirs. His father's friend, the deputy director of food and supplies, was shot at in the office. Then their neighbour, a chartered accounting student, was shot dead while playing carrom in his house. A Pandit auto driver, who was the only fully able-bodied person in his family, was shot dead too. Now that there were no patterns to the killings and panic had started in their locality, all Pandits were discussing possible next steps, and in consultation with their Muslim neighbours, it was decided that it would be better to leave for the time being. With uncertainty prevailing and no guarantees of safety, it was seen as the best course of action.

Thinking about the heightened tensions and rampant rumours during that period, Vivek recalls a particular incident clearly. As tensions peaked in the city, a message was sent across Pandit households that Muslims were planning an organized loot of their homes, advising them to be prepared for it. Vivek lived in a joint family, so his uncles started preparing. Measures were taken to protect women and valuables, including passing an electric current through the iron gate to deter attackers. Young Vivek, armed with his cricket bat, started making rounds of the house to defend his family.

However, after half a day passed and no one showed

up, he started getting bored and restless. He went up to his uncles, innocently enquiring, 'Khabar czer kyaze govukh (Wonder why they are late).' Shrieks of 'daffa khas yeti (get lost)', 'pagal gomut (he has lost his senses)', and Kashmiri curses followed, and he was thrown out of the house. Bored, he went to his Muslim neighbour's house, and he saw similar scenes of panic there. It turned out they had heard similar rumours that the armed forces were planning an organized loot of the Muslim houses, and only Pandits would be spared. So they were considering relocating the women and their valuables to Vivek's house.

While Vivek's family was contemplating moving out of Kashmir for some time, an incident in their locality shook them to the core. During the dheel period of one of the curfew days, his uncle along with his one-year-old child went out to purchase some essentials. A man approached them and angrily ordered him to go back inside the house. Moments later, a Muslim neighbour of theirs who was coming back home was taken out of his car and shot.

The previous night, some protestors who had been running away from armed forces had tried to seek refuge in their neighbour's house, but he had refused to open the door despite their desperate knocking. The random and gruesome nature of killings made even passers-by very hesitant to help the victims for they would face retaliation from outfits and agencies. With schools unlikely to reopen anytime soon, Vivek's family, like many others, decided to leave for Jammu, hoping to return in a few months. The next time Vivek would enter the city would be ten years later, in 1999.

At the beginning of our conversation, I had asked him what feelings Srinagar invoked in him. Almost without a pause, he said, 'Ironically it is the idea of being cocooned in a safe place; it is the place most familiar to me on the face of the earth. These feelings are not just a function of space but of people.' It was possible for him to feel this way about a homeland that he was forced to migrate out of because he was able to maintain a sense of connection with people at home. His father's friends would visit them in Jammu, and they started checking up on their well-being. He found friends in Kashmir with whom he didn't share life experiences growing up, but shared a common vision for their homeland and their place in it. 'I love Kashmir and when I say that, it means the people. Trying to sympathize with me, a journalist once said to me, "We understand your longing for Kashmir, for all the hills, rivers, and the landscape." But I don't love Kashmir for these things. They are there incidentally. Had they not been there, I would have felt the same. I am connected to people, not the landscape.'

I met Gohwar and Vivek a day apart, and in both their personal accounts of pain, loss, and suffering, there was an acknowledgment of the pain of the other. In their narratives, the experiences of pain don't compete against each other; they don't downplay the experiences

city as memory

of the other to amplify their own suffering. These should have been easy admissions for a place as broken as ours, where people let out a wail of pain even in their deep sleep, and one wonders what part of our collective history is haunting them. It should be possible to admit that different kinds of pain have existed side by side in Kashmir, leaving scars on our memories and bodies. It should also be possible to acknowledge the multiplicity of this suffering without pitting different pains against each other. Vivek simplified the process of mutual acknowledgment in a sentence for me, 'Che te peuv taavan, mai te peuv tavan. *A curse fell on you, and a curse befell me.*'

CHAPTER 4

PALE HANDS THAT LOVE BESIDE THE SHALIMAR

The year 1989 marks a point of rupture in the collective memory in Kashmir. For those like me, who were born during the tehreek and were too young to realize the magnitude of it, it has existed as a reference point against which all our experiences of history, nationalism, normalcy, public space, leisure, and mobility in Kashmir are measured and talked about. The perception of time exhibits a polarity too, in how it was experienced before the tehreek and after it. Commenting on the profound nature of changes that the political conflict has had on the socio-cultural life in Srinagar, Sameer Hamdani observes how it was during the 1990s and its aftermath that Srinagar became more inward-looking and suspicious. In the face of collective distrust and an immediate need for self-preservation, the city fractured into a collection of self-isolated and self-contained units. While linked by daily utility and need, there was no cohesion between the parts of the city as a whole. The social life in the city broke down into smaller disconnected fragments, and people developed linear zones of safety for themselves which stretched from the place of their residence to the place of their work. All interactions with the city were confined to

city as memory

these zones. The movement within the city became very service-based, and people travelled only when it was necessary. For those of us born during or after the insurgency, we learned to navigate public spaces in Kashmir within the scope of these limitations. For us, the idea of public places has always been inextricably linked with precarity and unpredictability. Excessive militarization in civilian spaces has led to apprehensions over the safety of vulnerable groups like women, boys, and young men, which in turn has translated into increased familial censorship and control over the daily movement of such individuals. Stepping out into the public spaces in Kashmir has meant the risk of getting caught in encounters, protest demonstrations, cross-firing, tear gas shelling, pellet firing, and so on. Bad timing is all that stands between a normal day and a life-altering tragedy, and life in Srinagar, like the rest of Kashmir, has learned to function within the confines of this precarity.

Present generations in Kashmir risk assuming that violence and repression are all our land has ever known. The scale and continuity of shared trauma have resulted in a sort of collective amnesia about Kashmir's history before 1947 and the 1990s. The history before the past seventy years seems distant and irrelevant in the face of continuing turmoil in the valley. If it wasn't for the stories from Kashmir's past which seep into everyday conversations through intergenerational accounts, we would have not gotten a peek into what life was like in the region before fear, violence, and pain became the overarching reality for us, overshadowing the gamut of emotions and experiences that normal people in normal cities experience. Always starting with tehreek brouh (before the tehreek), these intergenerational accounts narrate stories of Kashmir, including those of social and public life in the city, whose setting differs drastically from our lived militarized reality. It makes us realize the grave impact that the political instability and the subsequent militarization of civilian areas and public spaces have had on the social life and cultures of recreation and leisure in the valley.

Going to mountains, meadows, springs, parks, and shrines to unwind has been a cultural tradition dear to Kashmiris for many centuries. Walter Lawrence comments on the city's distinctive public culture of leisure during his time in Srinagar, adding that given the limited common public or civic spaces along the riverfront, particularly in densely populated mohallas, city residents forged a tradition of daylong picnics in Srinagar's gardens. He mentions the popular boat journeys on the Dal Lake that persisted until the mid-twentieth century and highlights the widely celebrated spring festivals in Badamwaer and the mulberry feast at Maisum. References to flower festivals being attended by crowds of men, women, and children are evident in other historical accounts of the city as well as cultural memory. For centuries, the open ground at Eidgah has been hosting numerous religious gatherings and annual festivals, establishing itself as the

city as memory

cultural and religious epicentre of the city.

The breakdown of the socio-political order in the 1990s practically led to the disappearance of these cultural traditions from our lives. When I hear stories of my parents and grandparents' youth, the Kashmir which forms the backdrop of their settings is more outward-looking, conducive to social life, and better connected with the world around it. I am aware that these nostalgic accounts of the past tend to gloss over the more painful and problematic parts of their lives. Still, hearing stories about the times when they would pack their food and set off in cars, buses, and tongas to picnic at Kashmir's famous meadows, streams, and shrines, and then return at midnight, I feel a sense of rage and pity for the present generations, thinking how our lives have been robbed of these seemingly mundane pleasures of normalcy.

It is important to remember that the absence of active political turmoil did not mean that different forms of social divides did not exist in Kashmir. Leisure activities have been predominantly a pursuit of the elites, and more specifically urban elites. Given the difficulties of transportation and connectivity in Kashmir prevalent till the twentieth century, the concept of picnics, which involved travel for non-utilitarian purposes and solely for recreation, was not accessible for people living in non-urban settings and for those who did not belong to well-off families. In such cases, religion acted as a motivating factor behind their travels; so a lot of people from rural areas would flock to the shrines of Dastgeer Sahib, Naqshband Sahib, Maqdoom Sahib, and Hazratbal, especially on the days of the urs. They also visited mosques like the Hazratbal, Khanqah-e-Maula, and Jamia Masjid, packing food with them which would be consumed in the parks and gardens located within the compounds of these religious sites. Exploration of the city for loitering, shopping, and sightseeing acted as an auxiliary function from these primarily religious trips.

Even before the rise of more urbanized forms of leisure and recreation in the valley, gardens and parks have featured prominently in accounts of Kashmir's public cultures since the earliest records of its history. G. M. D. Sufi traces the earliest references to gardens in Kashmir to old Buddhist literature and Sanskrit plays, stating that the sacred groves around the Buddhist shrines were probably among the earliest forms of gardening in Kashmir. During Kashmir's Hindu rule, a range of gardens, influenced by the concept of ancient Indian vatikas, were present across the valley, and they formed the setting for many ancient myths and epics. Among the earliest of such gardens in Hindu Kashmir was the Bagh-i-Tut or mulberry garden located near present-day Maisum. The garden was later maintained by succeeding Muslim rulers and is said to have existed way down till the late nineteenth century in a much modified form. During the rule of the Muslim sultanate, Zain-ul-Abidin is said to have planted gardens wherever he went. Four of his gardens, Bagh-i-Zainagar, Bagh-i-Zainadab in Naushahr, Bagh-i-Zainapor, and Bagh-i-Zainakot were particularly famous, but they cannot be found now. The Chak dynasty is also said to have created famed gardens, the Bagh-i-Husain Shah and Bagh-i-Yusuf Shah, but they too remain untraceable. It was the Mughals who undertook the large-scale landscaping project in Kashmir, which is why the traditions of Central Asia and Persia are the most visible influence on the present gardens of Kashmir.

Akbar visited Kashmir three times in his lifetime, and he was accompanied by his son, Jahangir, during two out of his three visits. Kashmir deeply influenced Jahangir who spent a significant portion of his reign in the valley, often accompanied by his queen, Nur Jahan. The couple, along with the Mughal court, would leave Lahore in March or April and reach the valley by May to escape the scorching heat of the plains. Feisal Alkazi states the frequency of their visits to Kashmir is said to have led to the circulation of jokes that the court was either in Kashmir, travelling to Kashmir, or packing or unpacking from a trip to Kashmir. Of Jahangir's obsession with Kashmir, it is said that he declared that he would rather be deprived of every other province of his mighty empire than lose Kashmir. Notably, Jahangir is said to have conceptualized the layout of the Shalimar Bagh, along with Shah Jahan, who collaborated with him on its design while he was still a prince. Like all other Mughal gardens on Kashmir, Shalimar Bagh was primarily an encampment site for the visiting Mughal emperor and his vast entourage. Nishat Bagh, another notable Mughal garden, was commissioned by Asaf Khan, Shah Jahan's father-in-law, in 1626. An interesting tale follows the construction of this garden. Despite Shah Jahan expressing his explicit desire to have the garden, Asaf Khan refused to gift it to him. This refusal led to a dispute between Asaf Khan and the emperor. In retaliation, Shah Jahan cut off the water supply to the garden, causing the fountains and water cascades to fall silent until the disagreement was resolved. Originally, the twelve terraces of Nishat Bagh were designed to symbolize the signs of the zodiac. The garden's approach was through the Dal Lake, and it is said that the waters of the lake once touched the last terrace, which now has a motorized road running through it. Deriving its name from the gentle breeze that blew under its trees, Shah Jahan also laid out the Nasim Bagh in 1635 which is now the popular Chinar Bagh within the Kashmir University campus.

After the Mughal rule, there was a considerable decline in the administrative use of gardens, and the successive Afghan, Sikh, and early Dogra rulers didn't pay much attention to their maintenance. It was during the Dogra reign in Kashmir that the region's culture of gardens was resuscitated with the establishment of the British Residency. Due to their alliance with Dogra kings, the British officials looked on Kashmir favourably and popularized the idea of Kashmir as a summer retreat. The city with its gardens and lakes was being transformed to cater to the influx of foreign visitors who sought refuge from the scorching summer temperatures on the plains. Feisal Alkazi notes how British officials sought to recreate familiar aspects of their homeland within their colonies. The hill stations in India, with their climate resembling that of Britain presented an ideal opportunity for these ventures. Srinagar, like other popular hill stations, became a preferred destination for health resorts aimed at providing the British with a sense of 'home away from home'. These resorts focussed on offering familiar cuisine, architectural styles, and infrastructure, creating an environment that would evoke a comforting and familiar atmosphere for British residents.

The colonial writings on Kashmir, in the form of travelogues, poetry, and fictional writing played a vital role in piquing the interest of the British in Kashmir in the nineteenth century. Widely popular works in Britain like François Bernier's *Travels in the Mogul Empire A.D. 1656–1668* and Thomas Moore's *Lalla Rookh* popularized the idea of Kashmir, the latter terming it 'the vale of Cashmere' and describing the region as 'the most lovely country under the sun'. Such narratives helped shift the tourist gaze of the British leisured class towards Kashmir. Amongst this crowd, there were some prominent photographers like Samuel Bourne and Fred Bremner whose photographs of Kashmir's landscape further contributed to the allure and fascination surrounding the valley in Britain.

÷

Since Yusuf Shah Chak's arrest and imprisonment by the Mughals in 1586, Kashmir has seen a continuous stream of foreign rulers over its territory. Much of what we know of Kashmir during these historical periods has been written through the lens of these outsiders, and in their accounts, the figure of the local Kashmiri, their narratives and experiences are completely overlooked. As noted by historian Mridu Rai, 'a large chunk of travel literature quite unfairly left out the people while elaborating on the landscape. Where it included the people, they were projected as inharmonious with the proverbial beauty of the land. Despite all admiration expressed for the natural beauty of Kashmir, Kashmiris themselves seemed invariably to be wanting in their appraisement.'

Different areas of the city were preferred by different ruling regimes, but owing to the strategic and military benefits of the area around the Haer Parbat, which allows a panoramic view of the city and easy access to the waterway network via the Dal Lake, Nigeen Lake, and Jhelum, this part of Srinagar found favour with almost all regimes that have ruled over Kashmir. Historically, all rulers have laid their claim on this natural spectacle, and the capture of this iconic stretch with the view of the Zabarwan mountain range and the Dal Lake has meant the symbolic capture of the city and the valley. From this elevated vantage point, rulers behold Srinagar's sprawling landscape, with indigenous Kashmiris appearing almost as incidental figures. Their aspirations for their homeland are perceived as marginal, and their purpose is merely to placate and reassure the rulers of their goodwill in their imperialist missions. The impact of the colonial presence on local ecological practices, socio-cultural traditions, and affective relationships that indigenous communities have had with their land has completely been written out of Kashmir's documented history.

The cultural influence of the British Residency in Kashmir outlived its physical presence. The vision that shaped the transformation of Srinagar into an urban centre was borrowed heavily from the colonial imagination of an ideal city. British aesthetic sensibilities shaped many cultural changes in the city: restructuring of Residency Road as a space for social and market activity that allowed the British officers to interact with local businesses and craftsmen, the use of Bund Road along the Jhelum as a promenade of sorts where British tourists and elites from the city would come for leisurely walks, and vacation practices in Dal Lake where visitors would stay in houseboats for months together, closely interacting with the Haenz community. The deep ties of this exchange can be gauged from the signboards of shikaras and houseboats in Dal Lake, most of which still bear British names.

Neerja Mattoo, a prominent figure in the Kashmiri literary world, was born just a few years after the British

Residency in Kashmir ended due to India's independence and Kashmir's accession to India. As an eminent teacher and translator, she has had firsthand experience of witnessing the evolving landscape of Srinagar. I visited Neerja at her Srinagar residence on a pleasant day in May. The first time we spoke on the phone, she had been very amicable and pleasant. After answering some of my questions, she had paused and asked me if I was a Kashmiri. When I had replied in the affirmative, she immediately switched to Kashmiri and chided me for not speaking in Kashmiri. Then, standing at her doorstep in Srinagar, I mentally translated my questions into Kashmiri to avoid repeating the same mistake. However, my attention was suddenly drawn to the security post at her front door and the men in khaki uniform who were observing me closely.

Born in a small locality near Exchange Road, Neerja Mattoo would go on to teach different generations of Kashmiri women at the Government Women's College for over thirty years. When she was born, the college building used to be the widows' palace, home of the old Dogra widows from the royal family. When the last of them died in 1950, it was used as the residential quarter for the principal of Amar Singh College, Dr M. D. Taseer, who was from Punjab, Lahore. Interestingly, during that time, the building also hosted Faiz Ahmad Faiz and Allys George, who had gotten married in a nikkah ceremony performed by Sheikh Abdullah at Pari Mahal. Neerja joined the college in 1952, two years after it was set up. Before this, S. P. College was the only place for higher education in Kashmir, and due to it being a co-educational space, it was out of the question for a lot of women. In her own family, her elder sister was not allowed to go to college despite her father and father-in-law being professors at the college and the campus being located less than five minutes from their house.

The early years of Neerja's youth coincided with Srinagar's stride with urbanization. Her close proximity to what was being developed as the Civil Lines area in the 1940s, along with her affluent background and cultural capital, ensured that she had the means and the exposure to experience the infrastructural and cultural changes that were taking place in the city. Her father had relocated to Civil Lines from Safa Kadal before she was born. While he maintained the strictness and control expected of a patriarchal figure from a traditional and 'respectable Kashmiri family', he encouraged his children to attend cinemas to watch Western films. Neerja recalls that since her father taught English at S. P. College, he was a bit of an anglophile, leading him to take them to nearby theatres like Regal Cinema, Amrish Cinema, and Palladium, all within walking distance from their home, to immerse them in the English language and culture. Regal Cinema, in particular, often showcased English-language films. To attract audiences, the movie titles were translated into Urdu and displayed outside the hall. For instance, when *The Brothers Karamazov* was released in 1958, its Urdu translation, *Kamraj Ke Bhai*, was prominently featured on the poster. Neerja fondly remembers watching films like *Marie Antoinette* and *Queen Christina* in the ladies' galleries of these theatres with her college girlfriends. Despite many Kashmiris not understanding English, they still attended these screenings to partake in the modern, urban experience offered in the heart of Srinagar.

Her living memory of the city allows Neerja to juxtapose the current Srinagar with the Srinagar of her childhood, and during our conversation, it was overwhelming for both of us to realize how much Kashmir had changed within her lifespan. She recalled the changes in the infrastructural map of the city, how the Usman Zanana Park which was established in 1920 for the women in purdah during the maharaja's time was taken over by the secretariat complex in 1960; how Gole Bagh, which held numerous circus performances in Srinagar and was renamed Gandhi Park after Mahatma Gandhi's assassination in 1948, was subsumed by the High Court complex; and how Polo Ground and Pratap Park were systematically shrunk in size. She fondly spoke of the times when water in the Dal Lake and Jhelum was clean enough for consumption, and they would use it to make food in their dongas during their overnight trips to Kheer Bhavani. When Lal Chowk was establishing itself as the hub of major political developments in the valley, it was used to hold meetings that were attended by iconic figures of Indian politics like M. K. Gandhi and Jawaharlal Nehru. When she would walk around Residency Road, all the latest books were available off the counters of the bookshops there. She recalled, 'One could get a range of books and magazines on Residency Road, from Vladimir Nabokov's controversial *Lolita* to Kate Millet's revolutionary *Sexual Politics*, you get it all in Srinagar till the 1980s. We were aware of what was happening out in the world because of these bookshops, the radio, and the kinds of people who we would get to interact with. We were not surprised by the people who were non-Kashmiris or different from us, because the city used to be filled with tourists. Even when the hippies came, we accepted them, and we would call them "gareeb angreez". All kinds of people would come here, we had opportunities to meet them and interact with them. Until 1989, it was very uncommon to see burkhas in public spaces, and a lot of Muslim women, particularly Muslim teachers, would also wear saris. Women's College was a very cosmopolitan space with a lot of diversity. There used to be professors from Aligarh, Lucknow, Punjab, Meerut, and Calcutta.' When I looked at her with visible disbelief, she proceeded to show me a picture of the executive committee of the student union of the Government Women's College, from 1955–56. She was in her final year; two Muslim ladies, Sakina Hasan, the vice principal, and Mehmooda Ali Shah, were dressed in a sari and an overcoat.

Then came the 90s. She recalls that between October 1989 and May 1990, the world around her had changed so quickly that she couldn't recognize if she were living in the same place. The period marked the beginning of something horrific, which kept getting progressively worse. There was an attempt to kidnap her husband in August 1991 who was then working as the principal chief conservator of forests. One day, as he was leaving his Gogji Bagh residence for a dental appointment, accompanied by Masterji, his Muslim driver, his car was stopped by two boys near the gate of Amar Singh College. The boys instructed both of them to step out of the car and demanded her husband accompany them as he had been summoned by their commander. Both knew what this meant, so Masterji engaged them in conversation, while her husband, a trained forester, made for his colony running for his life. Fortunately, he found the door of one of his Sardar neighbour's home open. He ran inside and bolted it. Unable to catch him, the two men gave up after a brief chase.

Neerja's husband came back home late that evening, and he was accompanied by men from the neighbourhood, who had all gone to check up on him after hearing about the incident. All of them sat with their family, reassuring them of their support and asking them not to leave. While all of this was underway, a huge group of CRPF and police personnel landed up at their residence inquiring about the incident. Because Mr Mattoo was an important government official, he was presented with the option of moving to a secure zone, someplace else in Kashmir. But he refused, stating that if he had to leave his house, he might as well move to Jammu like the rest of the Kashmiri Pandits. After some back and forth, he was granted security by the state, and the security post I had noticed at the entrance had been established there since.

Many of their neighbours were embarrassed after the incident. Before this, the dominant narrative in their neighbourhood, like many places in Kashmir, had been that Pandits were being sent away by Jagmohan Malhotra, the fifth governor of Jammu and Kashmir, so that he could get a free hand with Kashmiri Muslims, and people would firmly assert that there was no reason for Pandits to be attacked. For all the cases of targeted killings, most of whom had been the influential Pandits, people would weave some stories, some rumours would float about the victim having been a mukhbir (collaborator) or affiliated with some political party. But with Neerja's husband, the neighbours knew neither of these things to be true. He was attacked only because he was a Kashmiri Pandit. The next day a statement from the militants splashed in local papers mentioning Masterji and the Sardar neighbour's name, stating that yesterday their operation was foiled due to the interference of these people, and they had been severely warned. Thus, the whole city including her colleagues came to know about the attack, and there was a huge outpouring of support for her. One of her colleagues along with her husband, came with a very carefully written draft in Urdu to be placed in the papers. The write-up was to be from Mr Mattoo, and it would say that he is an innocent civilian who has never harmed anyone, and so should not be attacked. However, he refused to publish it. So, with the security placed inside their house compound, they continued to stay.

After the incident, Neerja continued to teach at the Women's College, dressed in a sari that marked her as a Kashmiri Pandit. The only change that happened was that she stopped walking to college and instead was dropped in a car. The college compound was her place of safety; however, she recalls that her colleagues would be worried sick on her part. She laughingly tells me, 'They used to tell me you have so many saris. Please give us a few, and we will get them converted into first-class salwar kameez for you. But I told them everyone in the college knows me, and if I suddenly changed my garb, that could look more suspicious. They might take me for an informer who is trying to spy on them by hiding my identity, so let me be. Everyone in the college was happy to have me, they would say all the Kashmiri Pandits left, but you have stayed. But we did it for our own reasons and not for some grand community feeling.' She recalls how at the beginning of the tehreek in 1989, when the leaflet prescribing abaya for Muslim girls and bindi for Pandit girls had been dropped inside the college compound, her students had laughed it off. A year later, when the gun commanded, they had to succumb. When the college finally opened in June 1990 and the students reappeared, there was a

city as memory

sea of abayas in the compound. The staff members too were fully covered, except for two women who made the concession through the dupatta on their heads instead of the abaya. She remembers how it was not just the abayas, religion had suddenly become important for everyone, including the students who now demanded a prayer room. Around that time, she remembers seeing a lot of posters springing up in Srinagar that would say 'Tajuub hai ki aapko nimaz ke liye waqt nahi hai (It's surprising that you don't have time to offer nimaz)' and 'Fakhar sey kaho hum Musalman hain (Say with pride that we are Muslims)'. She remembers witnessing a very similar spectacle during her visit to the Indian mainland a couple of years ago when she saw the masculine, angry poster of Hanuman, who has always been a jovial god in folklore and popular culture. Next to it read, 'Garv sey kaho hum Hindu hain (Say with pride that we are Hindu).'

As the interview time was running out for the both of us, laughingly she told me, 'If I tell you about Srinagar as it was in my childhood, it will only be a sad and depressing story for you. It was very different from the Srinagar you see now. These days, I am reading Salman Rushdie's latest novel, *Victory City*, and in the book, he talks about the upheaval in a particular place and how people were responding to it. So, when the bad times come to this place, some people decide to respond differently to it, and they choose to live in nostalgia. I too have decided to live in the Srinagar of my nostalgia.'

÷

One of the greatest tragedies for people like me who were born in Kashmir during or after the 90s is that we have never seen a version of our homeland that we can fondly reminisce about. The violent realities of post-insurgency Kashmir have always been so immediate to our everyday experiences that they become the primary framework through which we tell our stories. However, lives in conflict also suffer various other forms of social stratification based on gender, caste, class, disability, which tend to interact with the predominant realities of violence. This phenomenon affects the lives of some people more intensely than others. The journeys of young women in Kashmir have been shaped by stories, experiences, and threats of physical and sexual violence, and these perceptions have had adverse effects on the associations that they have been able to form with their surroundings and public spaces in the city.

Zainab Mir enrolled in Women's College almost sixty years after Neerja Mattoo, and by then, the turmoil in Kashmir had taken a different form. With that, the challenges that young women are facing in the city have changed considerably. However, the fight against patriarchal control of women's bodies and agency has continued to remain the same at its core. The patriarchal norms of respectability that were used to shackle Neerja's sister in 1952 and stop her from attending a college located barely five minutes from her house continue to be fully intact seven decades later, where notions of being a 'shareef ladki', a respectable girl, were used to dissuade Zainab from being in public spaces, even if at the cost of her education.

Zainab has been relying on public transport to travel from her residence in Downtown to Kashmir University and various other parts of the city. Throughout this journey, she has been actively monitoring how her demeanour and self-perception have transformed over the years. Brought up in a traditional Kashmiri Muslim family, she was drawn to religion from a very early age. In her teenage years, her behaviour was largely governed by the pre-existing notions of respectability, and she tried to live up to this ideal by shaping her conduct, clothing, and mannerisms according to it. Consequently, she became very shy and inward-looking. She also started wearing an abaya from a very young age, thinking that it brought her closer to that ideal of a 'good Muslim'. Even as she followed the normative rules, she had a lot of questions about her identity, religion, and morality. But people around her were quick to shut down these conversations so she carried this mass of unanswered questions with her when she went to pursue her degree in Mass Communication from Women's College. Finally, in a space where she was allowed to engage with her surroundings from a sociological lens, she found the vocabulary to articulate her doubts and think more critically about her own ideas of morality and the space of religion in her moral universe. In college, she was exposed to women from different backgrounds whose ambitions were unthinkable for Zainab, like pursuing a career in cinematography, production, direction, films, field journalism, or just the idea of studying abroad.

This experience facilitated changes in other spheres of her life. She recalls how she had enrolled herself in a darsgah (an Islamic religious school) to learn Quranic recitation. However, the head of the darsgah espoused a deeply patriarchal interpretation of the Quran and would say many radical things, sometimes going as far as asking her to leave her education. During a sermon, he told her as a 'shareef ladki', she should refrain from riding her scooty and instead take the bus. When Zainab expressed concerns about the persistent threat of harassment on buses, he claimed that enduring such harassment would earn her divine rewards for her patience. Even though she did not have the articulation to question him at that point, this struck her as a very problematic thought. She realized the danger of accepting ideas without critical examination, especially when they were cloaked in the garb of religion. She remembers this rejection as her first act of resistance.

Over the years, questioning and unlearning have become a part of her journey. Currently pursuing her PhD in media studies, Zainab has undergone a whole journey in self-assertion. As a young girl, travelling on the bus would fill her with dread and anxiety. She now takes the bus purposely to study how other women are navigating public spaces in the city. The probability of her being eve-teased on the bus is the same as it was seven years ago, but she feels more prepared. Over the years, Zainab took off her abaya too, considering it a significant performative act that symbolized both defiance and self-assertion. Many years later now, she is contemplating wearing the abaya again, but now she feels a heightened sense of agency and control over her decisions. 'I am contemplating wearing it not only in defiance of the broader Islamophobic discourse and a renewed understanding of why asserting my Muslim identity is politically important but also because I am trying to root myself in such symbols spiritually. I am trying to build anew a connection with my faith just for the sake of feeling closer to God. I am learning to place my need for God higher than all the political and social connotations that follow wearing the abaya,' she states.

Zainab and her friends are enrolled in Kashmir University, where they navigate everyday patriarchy and sexism like many young women in educational spaces. But the precarity of life in Kashmir permeates into their experiences in morbid ways. The day I met them for the first time, we sat in one of the gardens at Kashmir University's Srinagar campus. Nearby, a group of boys were playing cricket, and I was recording the interview. The ball from the cricket match kept landing in our circle, disrupting our discussions which ironically centred around the lack of leisure spaces for women in Kashmir.

Frustrated by the constant interruptions, one of her friends temporarily seized the ball, returning it only when assured it wouldn't come her way again. However, within minutes, the ball came back with increased velocity and struck one of her friends, who cried out in pain. In response, the women I was sitting with promptly rose and surrounded the men, leading to heated verbal confrontations. The woman who was hit by the ball, slapped one of the boys. In a surge of testosterone-fuelled rage, the batsman smashed his bat against the wall, causing chunks to become lodged in his arm, resulting in bleeding.

Tensions escalated further, and the idea of filing a complaint against the group of boys was suggested. As this was being debated, a bunch of his hijab-clad female friends, possibly their batchmates, started reasoning with Zainab and her friends, asking them to let the guy go, because if the complaint is filed, 'Isko pata nahi kis case mai gayab kar dengay (They might make him disappear)'—a reference to enforced disappearances in the valley. As the debate grew more intense, Zainab sat down, her fists clenched in rage. 'You know,' she said, 'we always find ourselves making concessions for men here. There are no mechanisms to hold them accountable. I used to have a stalker who would call my phone every day, hurling the obscenest things at me. So many times, I reached for my phone, ready to report him, but then I would hesitate, thinking about what happens to Kashmiri men in the police system here. Isn't

city as memory

it absurd that we are expected to show consideration to our abusers and perpetrators?'

Having completed her masters from Kashmir University, Saima Shakeel works as a journalist, and her experience reflects some of the uncertainties that the other young women shared. However, her struggles with identity and belongingness are intensified due to her unique living conditions and community ties within the city. Saima, along with a large portion of her extended family and community, resides in houseboats on Dal Lake and Nigeen Lake. This unconventional arrangement greatly complicates her day-to-day navigation of public spaces.

While women throughout the city speak of the scrutiny they face navigating public spaces, for Saima, each outing is especially conspicuous. Every trip to the city involves the elaborate process of procuring a shikara to 'cross the lake' to and from her home. These journeys, being so visible, inevitably draw more attention and consequently, invite heightened scrutiny and gossip within the community. She has been cognizant of these limitations since her childhood. Due to the distance of shops and the market from their home on the lake, even minor purchases became major undertakings. These outings required not only parental permission but also the arrangement of a boat to traverse the Dal. Given these logistical challenges, she and her cousins devised a game out of throwing coins into the water, often finding that easier than going through the hassle of spending the money in the markets. As Saima and her sister grew older, supported by their parents they opted to pursue higher education, but their choices raised eyebrows in their tight-knit community. The Haenz community still harbours reservations about formal education and exposure to the broader world. Many questioned the sisters' decision to study, with some explicitly suggesting that since their predetermined role was solely to prepare meals for tourists in houseboats, education would be wasted on them. So, when Saima began attending school and later college, the frequency of her crossings became a hot topic in their community circles. She explains, 'Once you're out on the lake, the idea is to complete all your tasks before returning. The fewer times you "cross the Dal", the better.' To minimize community chatter, Saima would strategically plan her outings. In one trip, she would attend school, tuition, and darsgah, and only then return home. Recurrent trips back and forth would be far too noticeable and invite unwarranted attention.

The community's indigenous lifestyle frequently finds itself under the attack of the state's Dal clean-up drives, which curiously coincide with election timelines and significant media events. Both in public discourse and official statements, the state and the wider society have unjustly attributed much of the lake's pollution to this community. This narrative perpetuates an ever-present fear among community members that their houseboats might be the next target. Adding to these challenges are the longstanding issues of economic hardships, disparities in education, neglect in basic civic amenities, and social marginalization based on their caste status, as well as their unique water-based way of life.

Reflecting on this, Saima reflects, 'What they want is for the Haenz community to diminish, to vanish, and ultimately to perish. Yet, it's bewildering because the very essence of tourism in Srinagar rests on this community's shoulders. We uphold everything that the city is renowned for. The shikaras, houseboats, and floating markets—all these iconic attractions are managed by the Haenz community. There appears to be a calculated strategy: to challenge the community's survival, appropriate and commodify our cultural assets, all while demonizing us in the process. They want the cultural symbols associated with our community to remain but wish the community itself to fade away.'

Over the past decades, Dal Lake's water quality has deteriorated considerably due to the inflow of untreated sewage from various sources like commercial establishments, residential colonies, houseboats, and municipal sewers. A 2016 study by the University of Kashmir revealed that only 20 per cent of the lake's water could be categorized as clean, with 32 per cent being badly deteriorated. The Haenz community bears disproportionate blame for the deteriorating condition of the lake, while the impact of untreated sewage from residential and commercial areas remains unaddressed. Official figures from 2017 reveal that out of the total daily discharge of 44 million litres of sewage into the lake, only 1 million litres originate from houseboats, challenging the notion that water-dwelling communities are the primary polluters.

Saima is particularly infuriated by the persistent stigma tying her community exclusively to water pollution. 'The water is our home. From a young age, we're instilled with the values of respecting our environment, with strict instructions against littering in the water or disposing of waste in it. A common childhood pastime we had involved patrolling the lake, fishing out trash, mainly wrappers discarded by tourists. We'd compete over whose section of the lake was cleaner.' What grates on Saima is the prevailing discourse that seemingly puts her community in the dock without a fair trial. The narrative tends to sidestep the accountability of the numerous commercial establishments around the Dal, failing to call them out on their environmental impact.

Amidst pressures from the state and the precariousness of their living conditions, the Haenz community is witnessing a decline in their indigenous way of life due to myriad reasons. Saima elaborates, 'A significant number of my relatives and extended family have already migrated out of the Dal Lake. Factors like space constraints and an increasing preference for privacy have played their part. From my observation, only about 20 per cent to 30 per cent actually remain in the Dal, with the rest relocating. Many are now setting

city as memory

up their primary residences in areas surrounding the Dal, like Taelbal, retaining their houseboats for guests or tourism. Raising children on the lake, with its unique challenges, can be demanding. So, it's understandable that many choose to move. The stigmatization faced by our community is especially evident during marriage discussions. Due to our houseboat lifestyle, there's a marked hesitancy from those outside our community to intermarry.'

Addressing this issue of caste-based discrimination that the community faces, Saima shared that many of her cousins choose to hide the fact that they live on the houseboat due to fear of stigma, but she proudly asserts her heritage. She clearly recalls an incident from her school days, when she was in eleventh grade. 'Our Urdu teacher would often say, "shor chu kara zan chu Haenz", implying, "You are as loud as the Haenz". At first, I let it slide, but as she continued, my patience waned. One day, I confronted her, highlighting that I belong to the community, but we aren't inherently loud. She was quite embarrassed.' Her face brightening slightly, Saima continued, 'I am aware of the stigmas surrounding our community and lifestyle, but I like the life that I get to live. Unlike most people in the world, my life is not confined by concrete walls. I get to wake up and experience the world from this beautiful lake, I get to read my books under the starlit sky. The water is our home and we care for it in sustainable ways. I think the life I have is incredibly special.'

÷

After the liberalization of the Indian economy, the idea of Kashmir as a tourist destination became more accessible for the emerging middle class in the Indian mainland. The political conflict affected the inflow of foreign tourists to the valley drastically during the 90s, and even three decades later, the inflow of western tourists has not matched its pre-tehreek numbers. The number of foreign tourists visiting the state plummeted from 600,000 in 1988 to 68,000 in 1989 and fewer than 5,000 in 1990. In its aftermath, there were increased attempts to make the valley more reachable for tourists from the Indian mainland, to assure everyone that *all was normal in Kashmir*.

Over these years, even as the ideas of leisure and recreation have become psychologically and spatially out of reach for the local populations, Srinagar is made to transition into a tourist attraction for outsiders. People visit the city looking for the Srinagar which they have seen in old Bollywood movies, in the advertisements from travel agencies, and on the posters from the government's tourism department. There is a map of convenience available for them as they drive straight through Boulevard Road onto the Nishat and Shalimar gardens, and their cameras focus only on the clean stretches of Dal Lake reproducing the chunks of the Srinagar that were marketed and sold to them. They feel reassured of normalcy, driving by endless lines of armed personnel and stationary army green vehicles, nozzles pointed at them, knowing very well they are not the target. Hopping from one attraction to another, this nature of exploration presents a very skewed map of the city to the outsider visitors, as it allows them to carefully navigate through the city's political history, years of turmoil, and the humanitarian crises, and see the city as a decontextualized landscape.

The 'tourist's gaze' is constantly used to design and market Srinagar. The Mughal gardens and the Dal Lake are packaged as unaffected chunks of paradise in the city that remain unmarred by political conflict. The tourists engage with their exotic notions of the local culture by recreating the caricatures that are sold to them through audio–visual propaganda in the form of photographs, videos, and other publicity materials. With brightly coloured clothes, supposedly traditional Kashmiri costumes, and prop kangris and jijeers, the tourists heartedly interact with the Kashmiri culture, while temporarily suspending their fear of Kashmiris demonized in mainstream popular culture. However, this conceptual suspension is only within the confines of these tourist attractions. Outside these bubbles of normalcy, the threat of the Kashmiri returns. This pattern is evident from the gaping absence of tourists from places like Maisum, Navyut, and other areas in Downtown, which hold important stories about the history and politics of the city.

While this kind of marketing is a usual affair for

tourist attractions, in Srinagar this is complicated by the fact that it contradicts the city's struggle to uphold its political identity as a city in conflict. A successful portrayal as a tourist destination requires Srinagar to give up on its existential demands; it needs to present itself as a city that is devoid of its historical trajectory, long-term conflict, and political aspirations. The local population, especially sections that are directly linked with tourism have found themselves conflicted about which narratives they should support because the situation places their economic interests directly in opposition to their political interests.

While these manufactured bubbles of normalcy are able to deliver the spectacle of paradise for outsiders, for the local population, the options to disengage from their lived realities are very limited. A consistent and repetitive reminder through which the conflict seeps back into a Kashmiri's everyday experience is the presence of the numerous military checkpoints placed on the route to all these tourist attractions. The symbolism of these checkpoints differs considerably for tourists and locals. For the former, they symbolize safe passages which allow them to navigate the 'violent side' of Kashmir and hyper-fixate on the natural landscape sapped of historical and political context. For the locals, these checkpoints are a cause of fear, anxiety, and often restricted access. Years of militarization of civilian spaces have rendered local parks unusable for most parts of the city. First after the insurgency, and then following cycles of protests from

2008, semi-permanent bunkers mushroomed around all open spaces where men would congregate for social, political, or recreational purposes. The deserted look of the Eidgah in Srinagar is a testimony to the culture of congregations that the city has lost over the past couple of decades. For women, public spaces for assembling or recreational purposes are practically absent, and even the little space that they had carved for their evening walks or morning walks in these parks was made inaccessible to them due to the presence of bunkers and the surveillant gaze of armed men.

Ifsha Zehra is a research scholar working on visual cultures in settings marked by protracted armed conflict at the department of communication at the University of California, San Diego. While she has been staying out of Kashmir for prolonged periods for her education, she is based in Srinagar's Lal Bazar and has been vigilant in observing the impact that the proliferation of military camps and bunkers has had on the social life in her locality, especially for women and boys. Where she lives, Khanbagh, was a famous park where young boys and men would gather for recreational activities, including local football and cricket tournaments, as well as political rallies. However, the establishment of a bunker nearby has rendered the park inaccessible for these activities. People have stopped visiting the park over fears of arbitrary frisking and the discomfort of constant surveillance. The women, who used to enjoy evening walks and engage in conversations with their neighbours outside the confines of their domestic spaces, also discovered that the space had become unsuitable for leisurely activities. This pattern has been replicated in various neighbourhoods of Srinagar, particularly in Downtown, further reducing recreational and community spaces in an already congested area. Speaking of her time in the city, Neerja Mattoo had described Bund Road along the river as a promenade where people would engage in leisurely walks and showcase popular fashion. But for Ifsha and her friends, walking through the same Bund Road and passing by the bunkers is an anxiety-inducing exercise. When they have to pass through that stretch, they don't loiter or engage in casual conversation, they sprint to evade the gaze of armed men.

Ifsha and her friends like to drive around the city, and their experiences provide glimpses into the nature of restricted access Kashmiris and specifically Kashmiri women have to many public parts of the city. She mentions the limitations she and her friends have faced trying to access many tourist destinations, such as the Shankaracharya Mountain or Dara. She recounted instances when they were turned back on their way to a mountain where they wanted to watch the sunset while the non-local tourists were allowed. She states, 'If it's just us women, I try to argue with them a little. I know, it would be futile but I still ask them why can't we go, and if we can't go, why are you letting them go? But it is always the same standardized response:

city as memory

"We have orders from above, we can't do anything, go back."' However, Ifsha admits that she refrains from arguing if she is accompanied by her male friends or brother, as young boys are more vulnerable and there is uncertainty about how the authorities may react. She never goes beyond Dara because her parents would never allow her, but even her male friends will not go beyond a point that they know will have a higher ratio of military personnel to civilians.

Many people like Ifsha pre-empt the discomfort that they may encounter on their travels, so they are unwilling to subject themselves and their families to the humiliating process of frisking at multiple checkpoints on the route to these places. Consequently, they are further dissuaded from venturing out. 'I have two young daughters and a teenage boy, who knows what they will do. Probably nothing will happen, but if anything unfortunate happens, what can I do? Who can I report to? What are the systems in place for something like that? I can't let my daughters go through such experiences. I will provide them everything they need but within the confines of my house,' says a shopkeeper based in the city.

These experiences are quite relatable for a lot of Kashmiris like me who grew up in a curfewed existence during the 90s. We were consistently reminded of the fragile nature of normalcy in our surroundings and urged to hold on to the safety that the confines of the home provide. These conversations took me back to the memories of my adolescence, when in my naivety I tried to force a happy memory in a city that was ablaze. It was the summer of 2010, and the valley was shaken by a series of protest demonstrations, first against the Machil encounter and then against the killings of civilians protesting the fake encounter. The schools had been practically dysfunctional, and like most of my tenth grade, in my eleventh grade too, I was getting to see very little of my school life. Confined within the walls of our house, each member had developed some odd coping mechanism to deal with time that had frozen. With the regular telecommunication blackouts, there was no way to remain in touch with friends or family. I had formed a habit of sitting at one particular corner of the drawing room, fixating on the one frame of the outside world that was accessible to me: a wooden electric pole with a solitary tungsten bulb on it. Day after day, I watched the skies change in the backdrop of this stagnant setting. Although I detested this frame, I found myself returning to it for it was the only marker that conveyed the passage of time to me in our stagnant world.

During one of the relative 'normal' days, I felt this overbearing heaviness in my chest, and it began to feel like I would die if I did not leave the house. So, I begged and pleaded with my father to take me out, anywhere. After skipping a few meals and persistently shedding tears at every mealtime, he reluctantly gave in and agreed to take us to Srinagar for a short trip to Mughal Gardens and the Dal Lake. Majid Bhaiya

city as memory

drove us from Varmul, carefully avoiding entering the city premises. Taking the Bemina route, we made our way through Batmalyun and Dal Gate, finally reaching Nishat Bagh on Boulevard Road. When we entered the garden, it presented a very deserted look, except for a few families and couples scattered here and there. The garden reeked of neglect, the water was not as clean, the flowers were not so prim, and the hedges were not trimmed. After a lukewarm picnic, we went for a shikara ride around Dal Lake, but the lake was covered in algae and weeds, and it smelled terrible.

As the despondent shikarawala rowed along the eerily quiet waters of the Dal Lake, tensions hung heavy in the air. Each sudden sound would make us tighten our grip on the sides of our shikara and anxiously calculate our proximity to the shore. In the midst of our journey, my father's mounting anxiety took hold, and he requested the shikarawala to turn back. It was unanimously decided that we should head home, despite it being only 3 p.m. After the stressful experience we had just encountered, I felt relieved to leave, weighed down by the guilt of having put everyone in an unsafe situation.

On our way back, we encountered disturbances in the city, causing our original route to be affected. We opted for an alternate path instead. The traffic came to a standstill, and people were in a frantic rush, honking incessantly. Due to the impact on National Highway 1, Majid Bhaiya chose to reroute and take the Sumbal route to reach Varmul. He bypassed the man from the armed forces who was directing the traffic. As we held our breath, he sprinted to stop our car, and dragged Maijd Bhaiya out, abusing and slapping him. Majid Bhaiya repeatedly apologized, and eventually, he was allowed to return to the car. As he sat back down, his left cheek and ear burned red. He tried to brush it off with a little laugh, cursing them under his breath. All of us remained frozen in our seats, and for the next hour and a half, not a single word was uttered. I sank in my seat, overwhelmed by a profound sense of guilt and shame, unable to look at the redness on Majid Bhaiya's ear, but aware that it was there, and it was there because of my selfishness.

÷

In a cultural twist of irony, the reluctance of families to engage in recreational and leisurely activities in the city due to safety concerns has transformed these hotspots into the preferred meeting points for lovers and friends in the valley. Away from the community gaze, and lost in the mixed crowds of foreign and local tourists, lovers and friends can be found hanging out along the touristy stretches of the city. Due to the prominent tourist presence, the Boulevard becomes one of the few areas in the city where people experience a sense of relative ease and freedom. Here, individuals are not constantly under the watchful gaze of the military or community, and there is no pressure to justify or explain their actions. It serves as a rare space where gatherings of young boys are not immediately viewed as a security threat and where couples can walk together without facing moral policing from communities. Atiqa and her friends from HMT feel that even though it is a hassle to get to these places from the other end of the city, Shalimar Bagh is the only place where she can spend a whole day with her friends. 'We could go to one of these uptown cafes, they are very expensive and we have to keep buying. They are intimidating, and we feel very out of place there.' However, she is quick to add a clarification, 'But we always tell our parents that we are going to Kashmir University instead of coming here, otherwise they will think we are *those* types of girls,' hinting towards girls who have boyfriends. She recalls a story of her classmate from school who had used her father's phone to call her boyfriend to fix a date with him in the Botanical Gardens—a popular meeting point among lovers and notorious for its scandalous instances of public displays of affection. The next day as they were sitting there, her father appeared at the garden out of nowhere, and both of them were thrashed out of there. Suspecting his daughter's affair, he had apparently turned on the call record feature on his phone.

Couples in the city have limited options to meet and interact outside the privatized public spaces like malls, restaurants, and cafes, and there is a strong class dimension that determines who meets their lovers there, and who meets in public gardens. Rabia and her boyfriend were regular visitors at the Botanical Gardens, during their six-year-long courtship, 'I know what people say about girls going there, but we live in Sopore and everyone knows everyone, so where are we supposed to meet? Thankfully the university is around, and I ended up doing a master's degree so that I would have an excuse to meet my boyfriend more frequently,' she chuckled. 'But it is really tricky to have such limited options. This one time when I was meeting him here, my elder sister ended up coming here for her school picnic and my cousin was here with her fiancé, and as luck would have it, we ran into both of them. They called my father immediately, and it was a whole thing, my father didn't talk to me for four months. It was very traumatizing for me then, but on the plus side that is how they found out about him, and now we are happily married.'

For many other women, defiance for love does not come so easy. Mehak has spent her life between Srinagar, Bengaluru, and London. She recalls when she was dating her ex-boyfriend, they always avoided meeting in the city because the paranoia of being seen with her boyfriend would get to her. She adds, 'It would be punishing for me to feel this way in the middle of my feminist awakening. I knew in theory that I needed to own my body and my space, but it was so difficult to do this in practice. This awakening works both ways, it makes you more aware of your social sensibilities, so there is heightened paranoia because you understand things more deeply.' She recalls how her boyfriend had arranged a little surprise for her at Char Chinar in the middle of Dal Lake, but given the stigma associated with couples being seen together, the whole journey was deeply uncomfortable for her. 'The judgement with which everyone, from the shikarawalas to people in other boats, was looking at us was just too much for me to have a good time. Similar incidents like this ensured that we never met in Srinagar but always outside Kashmir even though we dated for three whole years.' Similarly, Ifsha recalls how, during the lockdown in 2019, she frequently took walks in the Cherry Park near her house. On one occasion, she witnessed a chaotic scene where older men from the mosque were physically assaulting a young man. It appeared that the guy had been meeting his girlfriend when the men pounced on him. Frightened, the girl accompanying him had hastily fled, leaving behind her slipper. Ifsha attempted to locate her but was unsuccessful. She remarked that the missing slipper serves as a poignant symbol, representing the constraints placed on young people in love who dare to challenge cultural and religious sensibilities simply through their presence. For them, these gardens, where they can momentarily lose themselves and remain anonymous, offer fleeting moments of respite from the restrictive environment they navigate.

Opening her wallet, Rabia showed me a printed selfie of her boyfriend and her on Boulevard Road. The picture was taken in 2016, a tumultuous year when the city was engulfed in volatility, and the two had been separated by curfews, internet bans, and telecommunication lockdowns for close to three months. By word of mouth, both of them had managed to convey the time and location of their next meeting to each other, and fortunately, they reached Shalimar Bagh at the assigned time. The tourist count was low, and one could hear the sounds of tear gas shelling from a distance. It was a bizarre setting as people attempted to enjoy leisure while clutching their picnic baskets and belongings, ready to flee to safety at any moment. Everyone was alert, yet striving to prolong the happiness a little longer. Some sought to bask in the sun for a few more minutes, others clicked a couple more pictures, and families hurriedly devoured their lunch, trying to enjoy their day out.

For Rabia and her boyfriend, their journey back was fraught with danger. Their car had to evade stone pelting from protestors and endure verbal abuse from armed personnel. Upon reaching home, they bore minor injuries and a cracked windshield. I kept staring at the beautiful pictures of two young lovers against the backdrop of an empty Shalimar Bagh and a desolate Dal Lake, and it filled my heart with a pang of warmth to think that they did force a happy memory in a city that was ablaze.

ACKNOWLEDGEMENTS

One of the rewards of the excruciating process of writing is that you get to write a thank you note at the end of it. My heartfelt gratitude to Aleph Book Company for the love they showered upon my short story, 'Gobyaer', which was featured in two of their critically acclaimed anthologies: *The Greatest Indian Stories Ever Told*, edited by Arunava Sinha in 2023, and *A Case of Indian Marvels: Dazzling Stories from the Country's Finest New Writers*, edited by David Davidar in 2022. I am humbled by the faith Aleph placed in me when they entrusted me with this book. My deepest gratitude to my editor, Pujitha Krishnan, for her patient support, and for allowing me to choose the pace of my work. I also want to thank Vidisha Ghosh for her invaluable copyediting inputs.

For the support in writing this book, I want to extend my gratitude to Neerja Mattoo for the familial warmth I felt through our conversations and for her contributions to preserving Kashmiri short stories. I want to express my sincere thanks to Hakeem Sameer Hamdani, Dr Rashid Maqbool, Zareef Ahmad Zareef, Mariyeh Mushtaq, Ifsha Zehra, Bhavneet Kaur, Gowhar Fazili, Vivek Raina, Razia Bashir, Mohammad Faysal, Saima Shakeel, and Sadaf Masoodi, whose insights have immensely informed this book. I am grateful to all the individuals I interviewed, including those who chose to remain anonymous, that they graciously allowed me into their worlds and entrusted me with their stories.

This book has benefited significantly from the works of Kashmiri scholars and historians. I am particularly grateful to the works of Mohammad Ishaq Khan and G. M. D. Sufi.

My deepest appreciation for the love and support that makes that make my life meaningful, extending beyond the scope of this book: Badruzzaman Kairanwi, Barira Siddiqui, Anita Gurumurthy, Anhad Hundal, Mohit Srivastava, Shreya Mohan, Iqra Shah, and Asma Khan.

I want to express my heartfelt gratitude to Mohammad Muneem and Alif for their music. Their art has provided me solace and cathartic relief during some really difficult times.

My family has been a source of strength and inspiration; I am deeply grateful to:

My grandmothers, Saeda and Raja Begum, who were the first incredible women I encountered.

Fahmeeda Wani, whose love and basketful of dry fruits have helped me through all major life decisions.

Adhnan, whose unwavering support manifests in silent gestures. I deeply appreciate him enriching multiple drafts of this book with his comments.

Seerat, without whom I would have never written a word or learned how to experience the simple joys of everyday life. Her contributions have significantly shaped the ideation, research, fieldwork, and finalization of content for this book.

Saad, who makes love feel like the most natural thing in the world and forms the stable foundation on which my instabilities rest. His comments helped me simplify the language of this book and be mindful of exaggerations.

My father, Nazir, from whom I have inherited the love for stories and nature; and my mother, Mehjabeen, who taught me resilience can be kind.

And above all, Alhamdulillah.

NOTES

BEFORE WE BEGIN

ix	**The city, however, does not tell its past:** Italo Calvino, *Invisible Cities,* William Weaver (tr.), USA: Harcourt Brace Jovanovich, 1974, p. 11.
1	**In the essay Didion writes:** Joan Didion, 'Why I Write', *London Magazine*, Vol. 17, No. 2, June–July 1977.
3	**13.6 million people back home:** Babji, 'Jammu and Kashmir Population 2024', PopulationU.com, 8 March 2024.
7	**some rallies drawing as many as 20,000 protestors:** 'Eight killed as Indian Kashmir land row boils', *Reuters*, 12 August 2008.
7	**left around sixty-three demonstrators dead:** 'Amarnath land row agitation: SOPs flouted while dealing with protesters, says rights body', *Indian Express*, 21 June 2013.
13	**Jammu and Kashmir existed as a Muslim-majority princely state:** Ramachandra Guha, *India After Gandhi: The History of the World's Largest Democracy*, London: Picador, 2007, p. 75.
14	**One-third of the territory was attributed as a semi-autonomous entity:** Ather Zia and Javaid Iqbal Bhat, 'Introduction', in *A Desolation Called Peace: Voices from Kashmir*, Ather Zia and Javaid Iqbal Bhat (eds.), New Delhi: HarperCollins India, 2019, p. 12.
14	**Two-thirds of the territory:** Ibid.
14	**In 1949, UNCIP recommended:** Ibid., p. 13.
14	**Amidst these contestations, Kashmiris have long demanded:** Ibid, pp. 12–18.
14–15	**However, factors including alleged election rigging:** Manish Gangahar, 'Decoding Violence in Kashmir', *Economic and Political Weekly*, Vol. 48, No. 4, 2013, p. 36.

'IT'S PRONOUNCED SIRINAGAR'

19 It was on the Haer Parbat that Akbar carried out his first architectural intervention: Mohammad Ishaq Khan, *History Of Srinagar: 1846 –1947 A Study In Socio Cultural Change*, 2nd edn., Srinagar: Cosmos Publication, 1999, p. 9.

19 Later, from the mid-eighteenth century to early nineteenth century: Ibid., p. 12.

20 According to Hindu mythology, Haer Parbat was once inhabited: 'Visiting Hari Parbat (The Mynah Mountain)', *Kashmir As It Is*, available at kashmirasitis.com/visiting-hari-parbat-the-myna-mountain.

20 Just outside the Kaeth Darwaza (the main entrance): 'Gurudwara Chatti Patshahi Sahib (Srinagar)', KashmirHills.com, available at www.kashmirhills.com/gurudwaras/gurudwara-chatti-patshahi-sahib-in-srinagar.

21 The Haer Parbat Fort itself recently opened to the public: 'Hari Parbat Fort in Kashmir opens for public after 18 years', *One India*, 21 April 2007.

22 Srinagar was hosting the G20 Tourism Working Group meeting: Divya A., 'Third G20 tourism meet to be held in Srinagar on May 22-24', *Indian Express*, 7 April 2023.

23 Government officials had commented unironically: Peerzada Ashiq, 'Smart policing, slick bunkers for upcoming G-20 meeting in Srinagar', *The Hindu*, 20 April 2023.

23 The tiled stretch of barely 150 metres: Tariq Bhat, 'Kashmir's pedestrian market Polo View is a shopper's delight ', *The Week*, 24 May 2023.

25 The first traces of the name 'Srinagar' have been found in Kalhana's *Rajatarangni*: Khan, *History Of Srinagar*, p. 2.

25 According to him, Kashmir had several capitals: Ibid.

25 The remnants of Srinagari, 'the city of Sri': Ibid.

25 After the middle of the sixth century: Ibid., p. 3.

26 Successive rulers moved their capitals to other cities in the valley: Ibid, p. 4.

26 From 1320 to 1819, during the Muslim rule of Kashmir: Ibid., p. 6.

city as memory

26	Rinchan Shah (r. 1320–23), the first Muslim ruler, established Rinchanpura: Ibid.
26	Alauddin (r. 1344–56) founded Alauddinpura: Ibid.
26–27	Shihabuddin (r. 1354–73) chose area around the Haer Parbat as his capital: Ibid.
27	Zain-ul-Abidin (r. 1420–1470) established Naushahr: Ibid.
27	Sultan Haidar Shah (r. 1470–72) shifted the capital to Navyut: Ibid., p. 8
27	He championed religious tolerance: Shaista Amin, 'Zain-ul-Abidin, Budshah of Kashmir', *Kashmir Reader*, 14 November 2021.
27	As an arts patron, he invited expert craftsmen: Khan, *History Of Srinagar*, p. 49.
28	During the subsequent Mughal rule, the term 'Srinagar': Ibid., p. 6.
28	Yet, within Shahr-e-Kashmir, the Mughals created a distinct city: Ibid., p. 9.
28	Kashmir was a part of the Mughal empire from the end of the sixteenth century: G. M. D. Sufi, *Kashir: Being a History of Kashmir Volume I*, Lahore: University of Panjab, 1948, p. 241.
28	The Mughal empire's attempts to invade and control Kashmir's territory: Ibid.
28	The Mughal invasion of Kashmir initially met some opposition: Ibid.
28	The project of Kashmir held special significance for the Mughals: Ibid., p. 295.
28	Traveller François Bernier writes: Francois Bernier, *Travels in the Mogul Empire A.D. 1656–1668*, Archibald Constable (tr.), Oxford: Oxford University Press, 1916, p. 401.
29	Akbar's annexation of Kashmir through the disposition and exile of Yusuf Shah Chak: Sufi, *Kashir: Being a History of Kashmir Volume I*, p. 231.
29	The literal and metaphorical implications of this act: Basharat Peer, *Curfewed Nights*, New Delhi: Random House India, 2009, p. 134.
29	He often discusses the Kashmiri relationship with the

Mughals: Zareef Ahmad Zareef in conversation with the author, Srinagar, 11 May 2023.

30 'Sonas rupas karun dagul, maghul logum balaiye': Ibid.

30 With the Mughals settling in, their soldiers sprawled all around the city: Prithivi Nath Kaul Bamzai, *A History of Kashmir: Political, Social, Cultural, From the Earliest Times to the Present Day*, 2nd edn., New Delhi: Metropolitan Book, 1973, p. 388.

31 One of the theories proposed to explain the absence of worshippers: Khan Khanwar Achakzai, 'Pathar Masjid: A Brief History', *Medium*, 8 December 2020.

31–32 It was during the revivalist spree of the Sikh rule in 1819: Khan, *History Of Srinagar*, p. 12.

32 The floods of 1640–42 were so catastrophic: Mushtaq A. Kaw, 'Famines in Kashmir, 1586–1819: The Policy of the Mughal and Afghan Rulers', *Indian Economic and Social History Review*, Vol. 33, No. 1, p. 59.

32 The famine of 1745–46 is said to have wiped off 38 per cent: Ibid., p. 60.

33 Primarily constructed from wood, the city was inherently susceptible to fires: Khan, *History of Srinagar*, p. 24.

34 The dependence on the whims and idiosyncrasies of foreigners of brief authority: Walter R. Lawrence, *The Valley of Kashmir*, London: Henry Frowde, 1895, p. 203.

35 Afghans came to Kashmir in 1753: Bamzai, *A History of Kashmir*, p. 424, 428.

35 They not only displayed a complete lack of interest in public welfare: Lawrence, *The Valley of Kashmir*, p. 197.

35 Their reign saw brutal and mass persecution: Ibid.

35 Affluent Sunni Muslims were also not spared: Bamzai, *A History of Kashmir*, p. 424.

36 Pursidam az kharabiye gulshan zi baghban: Ibid.

36 It is estimated that the population of Kashmir plummeted: Ibid., p. 625.

36 Reflecting on the harsh treatment of Muslims by Sikh officials: Ibid., p. 611.

37 Sameer Hamdani, historian and design director: Hakim

Sameer Hamdani, *Shi'ism in Kashmir: A History of Sunni-Shia Rivalry and Reconciliation*, London: Bloomsbury, 2022, p. 56.

37 **These included shutting down the Jamia Masjid in Srinagar:** Bamzai, *A History of Kashmir*, p. 611.

37 **While Kashmiri shawls were receiving acclaim:** Khan, *History of Srinagar*, pp. 60–1.

38 **As a result, Kashmir was ceded to him for 7.5 million nanakshahee rupees:** Sajid Ali, 'How, on this day 72 years ago, Jammu & Kashmir agreed to become a part of India', *The Print*, 26 October 2019.

38 **In 1890, the Jhelum Valley Cart Road was constructed:** Khan, *History of Srinagar*, p. 35.

39 **Additionally, in 1886, the groundwork for municipal administration:** Khan, *History of Srinagar*, pp. 26–7.

39 **Wool was taxed as it entered Kashmir:** G. M. D. Sufi, *Kashir: Being a History of Kashmir Volume II*, Lahore: University of Panjab, 1949, p. 799.

40 **One of the earliest public expressions against Dogra rulers:** Tamoghna Halder, 'Kashmir's struggle did not start in 1947 and will not end today', *Al Jazeera*, 15 August 2019.

40 **By the 1930s, public discontentment:** Ibid.

40 **Tensions reached a tipping point on 13 July 1931:** Ibid.

41 **In 1965, under Project Gibraltar, state-backed insurgents:** M. Ilyas Khan, 'Operation Gibraltar: The Pakistani troops who infiltrated Kashmir to start a rebellion', *BBC*, 5 September 2015.; Sumit Ganguly, 'Explaining the Kashmir Insurgency: Political Mobilization and Institutional Decay', *International Security*, Vol. 21, No. 2., 1996, p. 80.

42 **Arms and trained militants from Pakistan started making the rounds:** Victoria Schofield, *Kashmir in Conflict: India, Pakistan and the Unending War*, 2nd edn., London: I. B. Tauris, 2003, p. 173.

42 **The period also saw Kashmir's largest minority:** Ganguly, 'Explaining the Kashmir Insurgency: Political Mobilization and Institutional Decay', p. 76.

42 **Large-scale protests and demonstrations erupted across the**

	valley: Schofield, *Kashmir in Conflict*, p. xiii.
42	**This was followed by a spectacular rise:** 'Getting Away With Murder 50 Years of the Armed Forces (Special Powers) Act', HumanRightsWatch.org, available at www.hrw.org/legacy/backgrounder/2008/india0808/india0808web.pdf.; Schofield, *Kashmir in Conflict*, p. 232.
44	**In just one year, the number of tourist arrivals had dropped:** Athar Parvaiz, 'Thousands lose jobs as restive Kashmir's tourism economy dwindles', *Hindustan Times*, 22 June 2017.

BETWEEN SHAHR-E-KHAS AND DOWNTOWN

51	**This was the first time eight-year-old Muhammad Faysal:** Muhammad Faysal in conversation with the author, Zoom interview, 19 April 2023.
52	**After Kashmir's conditional integration with India in 1947:** Praveen Donthi, 'How Mufti Mohammad Sayeed Shaped the 1987 Elections in Kashmir', *The Caravan*, 23 March 2016.
53	**Notably, from the 1940s to the late 1970s, differences over political ideologies:** Arshi Javaid, 'Seduction of the old City of Srinagar: An Enquiry into Competing Narratives of Belonging', *Dastavezi*, Vol. 5, 2023, p. 97.
55	**Experts attribute this mass euphoria to a string of significant geopolitical events:** Edward Desmond, 'The Insurgency in Kashmir (1989–1991)', *Contemporary South Asia*, Vol. 4, No. 1, 1995, p. 7.
56	**Even within this euphoric trance, it remained unclear:** Schofield, *Kashmir in Conflict*, p. xiii.
56	**In some areas, people had started symbolically burning Indian currency:** Sameer Hamdani in conversation with the author, Srinagar, 10 May 2023 and 13 May 2023.
56	**In other areas, people had stopped stocking up on food:** Bhavneet Kaur in conversation with the author, New Delhi, 20 March 2023.
56	**Militants trained in Pakistan and different locations in Kashmir:** Bhavneet Kaur in conversation with the author, New Delhi, 20 March 2023.; Vivek Raina in conversation

with the author, 2 May 2023, New Delhi.

56 **Operating as an armed political separatist group:** Mridu Rai, 'Kashmir: From Princely State to Insurgency', *Oxford Research Encyclopedia of Asian History*, 26 April 2015, available at oxfordre.com/asianhistory/view/10.1093/acrefore/9780190277727.001.0001/acrefore9780190277727-e-184.

57 **As weapons freely circulated in the market:** Manzoor Ahmad Reshi, 'Kashmir Insurgency: Its Changing Nature (1990–1995), *World Wide Journal of Multidisciplinary Research and Development*, Vol.4, No. 9, 2018, pp. 27–35.

57 **While the movement began as a centralized rebellion spearheaded by JKLF:** Schofield, *Kashmir in Conflict*, p. 145.; Desmond, 'The Insurgency in Kashmir (1989–1991)', p. 7.

58 **threatened against screening films in theatres:** Aijaz Nazir, 'Kashmir loses its cinema halls to prolonged conflict', *Al Jazeera*, 2 July 2018.

58 **It all arguably began on 19 January 1990:** Rai, 'Kashmir: From Princely State to Insurgency'; Ashok Bhan, 'Kashmir's Holocaust Day: Black 19th January, 1990', *Daily Guardian*, 14 April 2014.

58 **Approximately 300 individuals, seemingly selected at random, were detained:** Schofield, *Kashmir in the Crossfire*, London: I. B. Tauris, 1996, p. 242.

58 **A protest procession was underway when CRPF security forces opened fire:** Ibid.

58 **Estimates of the death toll ranged from fifty to hundred:** Mir Ehsan, 'Kashmir's First Blood', *Indian Express*, 1 May 2005.; Schofield, *Kashmir in the Crossfire*, p. 242.

58 **with some victims having been shot, and others, in desperate attempts:** Schofield, *Kashmir in the Crossfire*, p. 242.

58 **Subsequent events included the BSF firing upon 10,000 protestors:** Migrator, 'Jan 25: When 21 were killed for protesting against another massacre', *Greater Kashmir*, 26 January 2019.

58	resulting in twenty-one deaths and over seventy injuries: Ibid.
58–59	security forces attacking protestors in Zakoora and Tengpur Bypass in Srinagar: 'The day when army men fired 47 dead in Srinagar', *Kashmir Life*, 28 February 2017.
59	**the assassination of Mirwaiz Moulana Muhammad Farooq:** Muzamil Jaleel, 'The Mirwaiz's killing, and why it was a watershed moment for J&K', *Indian Express*, 22 May 2023; Safwat Zargar, 'An assassination, a massacre and the forgotten victims of a Kashmir tragedy', *Scroll.in*, 1 July 2023.
59	**In 1990, Kashmir had a documented record of hundreds of unarmed civilians:** Akhila Raman, 'India's Human rights record in J&K', Indiatogether.org, available at indiatogether.org/peace/kashmir/articles/indhr.htm.
59	**most localities in Downtown had their own local torture centre:** Schofield, *Kashmir in Conflict*, p. 170.
59	**Militants would seek refuge in the house of the locals:** Ibid., p. 268.
60	**Some people who had shifted to other parts of the city:** Sameer Hamdani and Mujtaba Kadri in conversation with the author, Srinagar, 10 May 2023 and 13 May 2023.
61	**I traced the spots from Father's shop to our house:** Farah Bashir, *Rumours of Spring*, New Delhi: Fourth Estate, 2021, p. 106.
62	**She recalls overhearing a conversation between her mother and aunt:** Ibid., pp. 37–8.
63	**She recounts a harrowing incident that occurred at her aunt's house:** Ibid., pp. 156–58.
63	**During the 1990s and its subsequent fallout:** Sameer Hamdani in conversation with the author, Srinagar, 10 May 2023 and 13 May 2023.
65	**Many interpreted this as a violation of Article 35A:** 'Amarnath land row agitation: SOPs flouted while dealing with protesters, says rights body', *Indian Express*, 21 June 2013.
65	**On a similarly large scale, controversy erupted in 2010:**

Muzamil Jaleel, 'Fake encounter at LoC: 3 arrested, probe ordered', *Indian Express*, 29 May 2010.

65 **The 2011 death of young Tufail Mattoo sparked a series of protests**: Ipsita Chakravarty, 'Kashmir unrest: Why are the crowd control failures of 2010 being repeated in 2016?', *Scroll.in*, 15 July 2016.

65 **Then, in 2016, the killing of local militant Burhan Wani**: Sameer Yasir, 'Kashmir unrest: What was the real death toll in the state in 2016?', *Firstpost*, 2 January 2017.

65 **a continuous curfew that lasted for fifty-one days**: Ashiq Hussain, 'After 51 days of curfew, restrictions relaxed in Kashmir valley', *Hindustan Times*, 29 August 2016.

65 **resulted in thousands of injuries**: Yasir, 'Kashmir unrest: What was the real death toll in the state in 2016?'.

65 **over 782 eye injuries from the reported use of pellet guns by authorities**: Billy Perrigo, 'Faces in the Darkness: The Victims of "Non-Lethal" Weapons in Kashmir', *TIME*, 6 September 2018.

65 **Kashmir witnessed a shift from militancy-oriented resistance to street protests**: Sanjay Kak, *Until My Freedom Has Come: The New Intifada in Kashmir*, London: Haymarket Books, 2013, p. iv.

67 **Along with the rise in casualties, this period also saw a significant increase**: Bhavneet Kaur, 'Everyday Suffocations, Smells and Sounds of Jung', *Himalaya: The Journal of the Association for Nepal and Himalayan Studies*, Vol. 40, No. 1, November 2020, pp. 20–29.

68 **'The people of Downtown have now incorporated'**: Ibid., p. 24.

72 **During the 1950s and early 60s, Bakshi Ghulam Mohammad**: Hafsa Kanjwal, *Colonizing Kashmir: State-building under Indian Occupation*, Stanford University Press, 2023, p. 2.

72 **The Civil Lines area on the city's outskirts, intended for the elite**: Dr Rashid Maqbool in conversation with the author, Srinagar, 30 May 2023.

72–73 **Moreover, with the rapid emergence of various militant groups**: Schofield, *Kashmir in Conflict*, p. 173.

73	**In the 1990s, the most economically disadvantaged were often the ones enlisted:** Dr Rashid Maqbool in conversation with the author, Srinagar, 30 May 2023.
74	**This narrative underscores its deep-rooted connection:** Javaid, 'Seduction of the old City of Srinagar: An Enquiry into Competing Narratives of Belonging', p. 108.
74	**The state has also been supportive of this through its Smart City initiatives:** Naseer Ganai, 'Visit By A Head Of State And The Controversy Over Shahar-e-Khaas—The Downtown Srinagar', *Outlook*, 27 September 2022.
75	**Moreover, this equation is complicated:** Ananya Bhardwaj, 'Changing face of Srinagar downtown —from education hub to graffitied stone-pelting hotbed', *The Print*, 30 September 2019.
77	**PAPA 2, a feared torture centre, was transformed into a luxury hotel:** Naseer Ganai, 'Srinagar's dreaded interrogation centres get makeover', *India Today*, 20 February 2012.
77	**Kawoosa House, are gradually being overtaken by commercial establishments:** 'Gore and Goss', *Kashmir Life*, 14 April 2012.
78	**Memorials established by the Association of Parents of Disappeared Persons:** Atty, Parvez Imroz, 'Monument of the Disappeared', DisappearedAsia.org, available at disappeared-asia.org/voice/dec_05/cs_kashmir.htm.
78	**Pandit mothers in cramped quarters recount tales of their houses:** Rahul Pandita, *Our Moon has Blood Clots: The Exodus of Kashmiri Pandits*, New Delhi: Random House India, 2013, p. 10.
78	**Years are marked by the most tragic events:** Migrator, 'Asiya, Neelofar rape & murder: No justice to victims as a decade passes', *Greater Kashmir*, 29 May 2019.; 'Rewind: A look back at 2010 Machil fake encounter case', *Indian Express*, 9 January 2014.; Najeeb Mubaraki, 'The Long Siege of Kashmir', *Economic Times*, 12 August 2008.'; Kamaljit Kaur Sandhu, 'How Burhan Wani was killed in encounter on July 8 last year: An exclusive account', *India Today*, 9 July 2017.

(UN)BELONGING IN THE SHAHR

80	The complete disregard for administrative and civic systems left the city: Khan, *History of Srinagar*, pp. 12–24.
81	Kashmir becoming the most militarized region on earth: Rani Singh, 'Kashmir: The World's Most Militarized Zone, Violence After Years Of Comparative Calm', *Forbes*, 12 July 2016.
83	Jahangir spent fourteen summers of his life in Kashmir: Sufi, *Kashir: Being a History of Kashmir Volume I*, p. 295.
84	Akbar is said to have constructed a great bastioned wall: Ibid., p. 248.
84	However, the city's construction did not affect the settlement pattern: Feisal Alkazi, *Srinagar: An Architectural Legacy*, New Delhi: INTACH-Roli Books, 2014, p. 61.
84	800 such gardens that existed in Kashmir during the time: Khan, *History of Srinagar*, p. 10.
84	Some noteworthy projects carried out by governors: Ibid., p. 12.
85	However, by the time of the late Mughals and Afghans: Ibid.
85	'The general condition of the city of Srinagar': Ibid.
85	In the absence of these: Ibid., p. 21.
85	Due to frequent cholera outbreaks: Ibid., pp. 22–23.
85–86	The water body networks were also severely affected: Ibid., p. 22.
86	Things were worse for the poorer quarters of the city: Ibid., p. 23.
86	killing 5,781 persons in Srinagar: Ibid.
86	5,931 in the other parts of Kashmir: Lawrence, *The Valley of Kashmir*, p. 218.
86	The city's expansion in the absence of state regulations: Khan, *History of Srinagar*, p. 22.
86	Referring to the state of disorder: Ibid., p. 26.
86	The general setting of the city was made more unsanitary: Ibid., p. 22.
86	In its earlier years, municipal action was met with severe opposition: Ibid., p. 27.

87	The municipality undertook the repair of roads and bunds: Ibid.
87	With the improvement in drainage systems: Ibid., p. 36.
87	With the road, the distance between Srinagar and Rawalpindi: Ibid., p. 34.
87	This was a major improvement for connectivity: Ibid., p. 33.
88	Consequently, the suburbs of Buchpur and Zaedbal were added in 1915: Ibid., p. 29.
88	Rural migration to Srinagar had been a trend for centuries: Ibid., p. 30.
88	Along with better civic facilities: Ibid., p. 30.
88	In 1901, the Srinagar Silk factory alone employed nearly 7,000 persons: Ibid., p. 31.
88	Commenting on the cultural implication of this change: Ibid., p. 31.
89	Nearby villages began to focus on dairy: Ibid., p. 31.
89	These shifts acted as catalysts for socio-cultural changes: Ibid.
89	The period saw Srinagar take steps towards incorporating features: Ibid., p. 35.
90	It also saw the inauguration of the land settlement and the reorganization: Ibid., p. 35.
90	By 1920, women in purdah would flock to Pratap Park: Ibid., p. 28.
90	The 1980s saw an increase in the outward migration patterns: Sameer Hamdani in conversation with the author, Srinagar, 10 May 2023 and 13 May 2023.; Gowhar Fazili in conversation with the author, New Delhi, 29 April 2023. Majid Maqbool, 'Urban Sprawl Uglifies Kashmir's 'Venice of the East', *Asia Sentinel*, 2 December 2022.
92	With the majority of the middle- and upper-middle-class populations: Sarbani Sharma, 'Labouring for Kashmir's azadi: Ongoing violence and resistance in Maisuma, Srinagar', *Contributions to Indian Sociology*, Vol. 54, No. 1, 2020, pp. 48–9.
94	Shamsuddin Araqi, a medieval Sufi saint: Shakir Mir,

	'Medieval Tyrants And Politicised Interpretations', *Outlook*, 16 April 2022.
96	With the larger democratization of the English language in the city: Dr Rashid Maqbool in conversation with the author, Srinagar, 30 May 2023.
97	A small population of prominent and educated Shia families: Ibid.
97	Economically well-off Shia families like these had access to cultural influences: Ibid.
97	So, while the cultural perceptions around Zaedbal: Ibid.
97–98	For instance, elite Shias from uptown found greater affinity: Ibid.
99	Sameer notes a gradual retreat of Shias from the city's public affairs: Hamdani, *Shi'ism in Kashmir*, p. 126.
99	After the 1830 riots, many Shias fled from areas: Ibid.
100	While historical sources predominantly attribute: Sufi, *Kashir: Being a History of Kashmir Volume II*, p. 799.
100	local narratives associate its popularization with Mir Sayyid Ali Hamdani: Sadaf Wani, 'Kashmir's Papier Mache Craft: An Archive of its People and Their History', Sahapedia. org, 27 September 2019, available at www.sahapedia.org/kashmirs-papier-mache-craft-archive-its-people-and-their-history#_edn7.
100	Most Shia families gravitated towards areas like Lal Bazar and Bhagwanpor: Sajjad Haider, 'Shias of Kashmir: Socio-Political Dilemmas', *Kashmir Observer*, 28 November 2012.
107	However, in the 1990s, as the state started coming down hard: Gowhar Fazili in conversation with the author, New Delhi, 29 April 2023.
109	This was happening in the broader context of 'catch-and-kill' policy: Human Rights Watch, 'India's Secret Army in Kashmir: New Patterns of Abuse Emerge in the Conflict', UNHCR, 1 May 1996, available at www.refworld.org/reference/countryrep/hrw/1996/en/32217.
113	Rahul Pandita makes a reference to how truths became different: Pandita, *Our Moon has Blood Clots*, p. 46.

PALE HANDS THAT LOVE BESIDE THE SHALIMAR

120 In the face of collective distrust and an immediate need for self-preservation: Sameer Hamdani in conversation with the author, Srinagar, 10 May 2023 and 13 May 2023.

120 The social life in the city broke down into smaller disconnected fragments: Ibid.

120–21 All interactions with the city were confined to these zones: Ibid.

122 Going to mountains, meadows, springs, parks, and shrines: C. M. Villiers Stuarts, *Gardens of the Great Mughals*, London: Adams and Charles Square, 1913, p. 175.

122 Walter Lawrence comments on the city's distinctive public culture of leisure: Lawrence, *The Valley of Kashmir*, p. 26, 241, 300.

122 He mentions the popular boat journeys on the Dal Lake: Ibid., p. 37.

122 widely celebrated spring festivals in Badamwaer and the mulberry feast at Maisum: Alkazi, *Srinagar*, p. 26.

122 For centuries, the open ground at Eidgah: Alkazi, *Srinagar*, p. 26.

124 G. M. D. Sufi traces the earliest references to gardens in Kashmir: Sufi, *Kashir: Being a History of Kashmir Volume II*, p. 524.

124 During Kashmir's Hindu rule, a range of gardens: 'Mughal Gardens in Kashmir', UNESCO: World Heritage Convention, available at whc.unesco.org/en/tentativelists/5580.

124 Among the earliest of such gardens in Hindu Kashmir: Ibid.

124 The garden was later maintained by succeeding Muslim rulers: Ibid.

125 Four of his gardens: Sufi, *Kashir: Being a History of Kashmir Volume II*, p. 528.

125 The Chak dynasty is also said to have created famed gardens: Ibid.

125 Akbar visited Kashmir three times in his lifetime: 'Mughal Gardens in Kashmir', UNESCO: World Heritage Convention, available at whc.unesco.org/en/tentativelists/5580.

125	Feisal Alkazi states the frequency of their visits to Kashmir: Alkazi, *Srinagar*, p. 58.
125	Of Jahangir's obsession with Kashmir: Ibid.
126	An interesting tale follows the construction of this garden: Stuarts, *Gardens of the Great Mughals*, pp. 168–69.
126	In retaliation, Shah Jahan cut off the water supply: Ibid.
126	Originally, the twelve terraces of Nishat Bagh: Ibid.
126	Deriving its name from the gentle breeze that blew under its trees: Sufi, *Kashir: Being a History of Kashmir Volume II*, p. 528.
126	After the Mughal rule, there was a considerable decline: Alkazi, *Srinagar*, pp. 70–3, 78.
127	Feisal Alkazi notes how British officials sought to recreate familiar aspects: Ibid., p. 78.
127	Thomas Moore's *Lalla Rookh* popularized the idea of Kashmir: Thomas Moore, 'The Light of the Harem', in *Lalla Rookh: An Oriental Romance*, London: Longman, Green, Longman, and Roberts, 1861, p. 285.
128	As noted by historian Mridu Rai: Mridu Rai, *Hindu Rulers, Muslim Subjects*, New Delhi: Permanent Black, 2012, p. 1.
129	The cultural influence of the British Residency in Kashmir outlived: Alkazi, *Srinagar*, pp. 76–8.
132	She recalled the changes in the infrastructural map of the city: Sanchita Raina, 'First Time in 60 Years: Civil Secretariat Building Srinagar Gets Exterior', *The Typewriter*, 13 July 2021.
132	how Gole Bagh, which held numerous circus: 'Numaeshi (Central Market) Part 1 by Zareef Ahmad Zareef', Post, YouTube, 22 October 2022, available at <www.youtube.com/watch?v=gBuy1avRZ6c>.
135	Before this, the dominant narrative in their neighbourhood: Neerja Mattoo in conversation with the author, Srinagar, 10 and 11 May 2023.
144	The community's indigenous lifestyle frequently finds itself under the attack: Shalini Punjabi, 'A Landscape of Multiple Emergencies: Narratives of the Dal Lake in Kashmir', in Frank Uekötter (ed.), *Exploring Apocalyptica: Coming to*

	Terms with Environmental Alarmism, Pittsburgh: University of Pittsburgh Press, 2018, pp. 150–68.
145	Over the past decades, Dal Lake's water quality has deteriorated: Deepanshu Monhan, Najam Saqib, and Ishfaq Wani, 'Kashmir: The Plight of the Hanji Community of Srinagar's Dal Lake Area', *The Quint*, 3 March 2024.
145	A 2016 study by the University of Kashmir revealed that only 20 per cent: Ibid.
145–46	Official figures from 2017 reveal that out of the total daily discharge: Ibid.
148	**The number of foreign tourists visiting the state plummeted:** Kenneth J. Cooper, 'Indian Forces Repress Kashmir Insurgency—and Citizens', *Washington Post*, 5 July 1996.